A Journey With

John Jacob Niles

A Memoir of My Years With Johnnie

John Jacob Niles
carving a door for St. Hubert's church
in Athens, KY
Photographer: Helm Roberts
Photo taken: 1970 ©

A Journey With

John Jacob Niles

A Memoir of My Years With Johnnie

by
Jacqueline Roberts
and Kerstin Warner

Jacqueline Roberts

Lexington
University of Kentucky Libraries
Occasional Paper No. 13
2001

Table of Contents

Preface

In this preface I want to introduce you to some of the principal characters to whom I owe such a great debt. Above all, I want to honor the memory of my dear friend Rena Niles. Rena served officially as the facilitator and business manager of John Jacob Niles' career, but she did a great deal more than that. Rena was a creative person, a talented writer, a woman with her own independent interests, who also had a gift for friendship and meeting the public. Rena managed a great deal more than tour arrangements and publishing negotiations. Her kindness and good will, her grace and diplomacy contributed to a working atmosphere that was extremely pleasant. We had been close friends all these years: I loved and admired her, and I was thrilled to sing at her eighty-second birthday party. Not long after that, Rena suffered a fatal accident during her daily swim. Not a day passes but I think of her.

I have also been blessed with wonderful accompanists. I have always joked that I find them in the grocery store. But I truly did meet Janelle Pope, now Dishman, at the Gateway in Zandale Shopping Center, and I met Nancie Field at the old A & P on Tates Creek Road. These two women, with whom I worked so closely over the years, understood the "duet" between voice and instrument that Johnnie's songs required. Janelle was my accompanist when Johnnie was in the process of writing the Niles-Merton songs, and she performed when they were first introduced to the world. Nancie Field became my accompanist in 1971 and remained so through 1988, during the period when we were touring and after. In both cases, they volunteered to work with me when they heard that I was planning a recital, and they made these offers during conversation in the grocery store. They too have been good friends and colleagues, sharing an important part of my life.

Johnnie always referred to us as "the girls," which did not describe us quite accurately, since we were mothers of elementary school children. He enjoyed joking with us and teasing us both onstage and off, and we didn't mind indulging him in this. We always felt honored to have been selected by him to perform his music, and we were in awe of him as a composer and performer.

For my musical education, I am grateful to my mother, Elizabeth Warnick, first of all. I also want to thank my sisters Jeannine Stephens and Ruth Trumbo, who have always been supportive of my work and helpful in countless ways. I owe a debt of gratitude to my cousin Charles Simpson, who made my beautiful dulcimers. I continued to be fortunate in finding wonderful pianists, and I particularly want to thank Claire Vance and Tedrin Blair Lindsay for the performances we shared.

I want to thank my sons, Bruce and John Roberts, for their patience in having a singing mother. Many wonderful baby sitters made it possible for me to perform and travel with Johnnie and Rena in the early years. A special "thank you" must go to Mary Tippie, for the wonderful food she prepared for us at Boot Hill Farm over the years.

Finally, I want to thank my husband Helm Roberts, who in addition to being wholeheartedly supportive of my work, willingly served as my photographer and recording technician. Without Helm's efforts this particular book would not have been possible.

I

We Meet

I was an undergraduate music major at Oberlin when I first learned about John Jacob Niles as a composer known for "I Wonder as I Wander" and "Black is the Color of My True Love's Hair," and many other songs— and equally renowned for performing them, accompanying himself on the dulcimer and singing in a distinctive high voice. I remember being proud that my home state of Kentucky had a famous composer and balladeer. But I would have never have believed you if you told me when I was a young singer that I would spend eighteen years of my life in a musical association, working and performing with John Jacob Niles, who was already well into middle age.

"Musical association" seems a little too formal for this long creative collaboration and friendship. When Johnnie announced, "You're going to sing my music with me on stage and before my friends," I was thrilled. My training and performance experience had all been classical. I loved the English and American art songs, though I performed Wolf and Schumann songs as well. Johnnie was associated with a very different kind of music. I could imagine myself singing, "Black is the Color of My True Love's Hair," and "I Wonder as I Wander," but could I carry off "Frog Went A-Courtin' and He Did Ride?" And when Johnnie eventually said, "You're going to learn to accompany yourself on the dulcimer!" I reacted with, "Oh, no!" I just could not imagine myself playing a dulcimer— I never saw myself as a folk musician. Johnnie's distinctive voice, his recordings, and his definitive song book placed him firmly in the popular tradition of musicians like Woody Guthrie, Pete Seeger and Burl Ives. I wasn't sure where I would fit in, but I did as he suggested.

For all his celebrity and fame as an American composer, or more likely because of it— sour grapes— there were those in his home state who looked down their noses at him. "Why do you want to work with him?" they'd say. "He steals his material and then passes it off as his own." These criticisms came as often as not from local academics: "He's not an authentic folk musician— he makes up songs and pretends that he collected them." "He's just an arrogant, self-promoting old fraud." I never took any of this seriously, because nobody knew any better than I how Johnnie composed music, and I never heard him say anything untruthful about his sources. He loved talking about his creative process: I think he was extremely proud to be composing and performing new material at his age.

Then there was the matter of working with such a consummate performer. His muttonchop whiskers and white jacket and tables full of dulcimers were as distinctive as his high voice, his Tall Tales and ad lib commentary. He'd held the stage as a solo performer for many years, and audiences adored him. How would I fit in?

I needn't have worried about working with Johnnie, for he persisted and taught me patiently and thoroughly. I learned to sing his music exactly as he wanted it performed. I even, after the initial reluctance, learned to accompany myself (not too well and not too happily) on the dulcimer. From the time that I met John Jacob Niles, my career took new and intriguing directions and my musical education never stopped presenting me with new surprises. I toured and performed with Johnnie frequently, under all sorts of conditions and in all kinds of places. Whether we were performing or preparing material, I felt that I was always moving along a path of learning, always exploring new territory.

Johnnie's youthful wanderings in the mountains of Kentucky, collecting music and musical instruments, had led him to this point— no matter that he was in his seventies and eighties— when he was ready to embark on a new kind of musical and spiritual odyssey. He now was experimenting with unusual harmonies and new purposes in his composition of vocal music, for he found these to be philosophically compatible with his new interest in Zen Buddhism and the fresh vein of poetry it inspired. Let me tell you how we met.

FIRST VISIT TO BOOT HILL

It all began with an impulse, my reaching for the telephone to call John Jacob Niles. I was in the process of preparing a recital of sacred music scheduled for the seventh of May, 1967, in the Second Presbyterian Church in Lexington, Kentucky. My program consisted in the first half of songs from my classical repertoire including Mozart and Hugo Wolf, but the second half was devoted to contemporary American composers— Ralph Vaughan-Williams, Samuel Barber and John Jacob Niles.

My husband and I had recently settled in Lexington, Kentucky with our two young sons. I had met John Jacob Niles one day when I sang at Christ Church Episcopal, where the Niles family worshiped. At an Easter Service I sang Niles' "The Little Family," and afterward I had been introduced to the composer. But that was the extent of our acquaintance. So I summoned up my nerve, reached for the phone and called him to ask this favor: would he please be so good as to suggest some material for my recital? To my relief, he was very cordial and gracious and promptly invited Janelle Pope, my accompanist, and me to the Niles farm, Boot Hill. "Come on out here and I'll show you what I've got," he said. Janelle and I hired a sitter for our children and set out for our audition.

Boot Hill was not far from Lexington. The house was not a grand plantation style manor, but it spread out over several levels as it had grown. The heart of the home was the big stone hearth which dominated the large room where music was composed and performed and where guests were entertained. Above the magnificent Steinway piano hung Victor Hammer's dramatic portrait of John Jacob Niles in the white jacket he wore for performances.

I'm not an architect, but my husband Helm Roberts is, so I asked him to describe this wonderful place. The rest of the paragraph is in Helm's words.

"The architecture of Boot Hill Farm reflected the life and work of John Jacob Niles, from its beginning in the mid-thirties to his death in 1980. The house "grew" from a pre-World War Two Gunnison pre-fab to an architectural manifestation of the life and work of the artist— serving as studio, recital hall, exhibition space, guest quarters and home. During the war a "Pony Barn" was built for the livestock at Boot Hill. Rena was an accomplished rider of the Iroquois Hunt, and their sons Tom and John Ed also rode. This structure was built of "rammed earth," reflecting the shortage of normal materials needed for the war effort. After the war, Ernst Johnson, a Lexington architect, was retained to design an expansion of the original home to include a dining/kitchen area, exhibit gallery and studio/recital room. Johnnie did much of the construction himself in this last project— the brick fireplace, the flagstone floor and carvings of the finished woodwork in the entrance areas. In later years, the Pony Barn was converted to Johnnie's studio."

Janelle and I were a little nervous that first day about running through the recital. Even when he was being informal and casual, John Jacob Niles was a "presence." All those years of performing his music had infused him with such a confident manner, and of course there was his charisma, and the luster of his fame. He had become an internationally recognized composer and performer and now, at age seventy-six, he was enjoying being a grand old man, proudly flaunting his seniority. Anyone under fifty could expect to be teased and treated as a mere child.

But on this day he was all business, no nonsense, intently focussed on the music once we began. His opinions were thoughtful and critical, and I could tell that he understood a much broader range of music than his performances and songbook might lead one to imagine. He suggested that I sing two songs he had recently written, "The Flower of Jesse" and "Come Gentle Dark." They were perfect.

"Now may I ask you a favor?" he said, placing a manuscript on the piano in front of Janelle. "I have taken a poem by Thomas Merton," he explained, "and made it a song for soprano voice. Would you sight-read it so that I might hear how it sounds?" We were pleased to do what he wished, and he listened intently to every note. The song was "The Messenger," in which the coming of spring reminds a sentry of the day of the Annunciation, "The morning the Mother of God/ Loved and dreaded the message of an angel:" I never dreamed, as we read our way through it, that I would sing this song so many times and in so many places. I was perfectly happy that day, to have been received so kindly and critiqued so helpfully. But now that I look back on it, there was something unusual about the way I acted on impulse, and even something portentous about the song itself, and the look on Johnnie's face as he listened to it: it was a kind of creative annunciation that would transform all of our lives.

Johnnie and Rena came to my sacred recital and sat in the very front. "The Flower of Jesse" was on my sacred recital program at the Second Presbyterian Church.

I repeated my "Sacred Recital" later that year at the Oakhurst Presbyterian Church in Charleston, West Virginia, where my sister Ruth Trumbo was living. Ruth has always been a wonderful support to my performing. If she was in the area where I had a program, she would be there. She has a real flair for entertaining, and I remember Ruth's lovely reception after the recital.

CHRISTMAS PARTY

It was around Christmastime that same year that Johnnie suddenly announced, "You're going to sing my music on stage with me and before my friends!" Janelle and I were pleased to be asked— urged— to be a part of the Niles Christmas festivities at Boot Hill. There was room for about forty people in the living room/ performance space: Johnnie and Rena borrowed folding chairs from the nearby Christian Church Camp. Johnnie was very much the center of attention. I remember him saying, "If they're going to come here and drink my liquor, and eat my food, they're going to hear my music."

My husband, Helm Roberts, with Johnnie's approval, brought recording equipment to this performance, and to many subsequent performances, and it is thanks to Helm's technical work that I have this wonderful record of Johnnie's comments as well as the songs themselves. Johnnie will hereafter speak for himself, in his own words, in his own style.

JJN: *This afternoon we have Jackie Roberts and Janelle Pope and my son John Edward, who will be here in a few minutes: he's going to play cello and the girls are going to— Jackie's going to sing and Janelle's going to play. Of course you know that I am a consummate egotist. I always present people singing my own music, and to hell with the hindmost. I know all about Bach, Beethoven, and Brahms: I've been*

14

exposed to it ever since I was knee-high to a duck. The first
music I ever heard was the great symphonic works of
Beethoven and Brahms. Now nowadays, notwithstanding—
come on over here, honey, here's a seat for you!

"The Flower of Jesse" is based on a poem written by a man I
respect enormously, long dead. He was a fifteenth century
poet, James Ryman— blind and deaf, the chaplain at
Hopemount Abbey in England. James Ryman's poetry is so
superlatively designed, and his understanding of what he
wants to say about Jesus Christ is so accurately put down in
words, I wonder why we haven't used him more. This is my
adaptation of James Ryman's poem written at the turn of the
fifteenth century

"The Flower of Jesse"— I wrote the text and the tune, and I
talked to the Bishop about it and he tells me it's a legitimate
thing, it's our Lord and Master Jesus Christ, of course, and
it reaches back into ancient Hebrew history— "There is a
flower sprung of a tree/ The root thereof is called Jesse"

All through this opening part of the recital, the Niles'
friends were arriving, removing their winter coats, signing
the guest book that "Miss Rena" kept next to the door, and
settling in. None of this commotion fazed Johnnie, who
simply picked up where he'd left off, as you will see.

JJN: Notwithstanding, at this age in my life, I feel that
I'm justified in presenting my own material. It's a little
bit different from the average run of music. My wife
even admits that my accompaniments are so superior to
the accompaniments one finds in the average music!
Now my son says that I write "romantic modernism."
Some of it bites quite a lot: it's dissonant, yes indeed, but
it always comes out somewhat even. All right— we start
with something that I wrote, and I have it down in the low
sexy part of this girl's voice. She's a soprano, but when you
pitch her down in the low mezzo area, you get something for
your money! All right, honey.

John Jacob Niles
posed with dulcimer before Hammer portriat
at Boot Hill Farm
photographer: Jack Cobb
photo taken: 1960 ©

At this point I sang "I Dare Not Ask." When I listen to the tape now, I can hear murmurs just before the first applause— a kind of an "Mmm!" of approval, but of course I don't remember it from the performance.

> *JJN: The legend of the robin and the thorn is an established legend in Spain; it has to do with the idea that the robins never did have any color in their feathers, and they went to God and they argued with him considerably. But he sent them back, and for generations after that they were all brown until ultimately one robin pulled the thorn out of Christ's crown. Blood splashed on his breast, and he's had a red breast ever since.*

People were still arriving throughout these early songs, and some were boisterously greeted— "It's JOE!"— right in the middle of Johnnie's introduction. I sang two of the dramatic narrative songs, "My Little Black Star, and "Incoming Tide."

> *JJN: The next song I owe to my father, God rest him, who took me along on a political junket. I was a very small boy, holding his hand: we came upon many very interesting colored people who were singing all kinds of music in the Reelfoot Lake area, and out of it all came a thing called "My Little Black Star," about a mother and her brood of children, and particularly a tiny one. The husband had gotten into some difficulty and was in the penitentiary. "Oh my baby is like a little black star/ He's just like his daddy way yonder far."*

> *Then in Boston, Massachusetts during one of my trips out there— I was to sing at Harvard or— I don't remember now— there was a newspaper article about a girl who'd lost her lover in a casualty at sea. The ship was sunk, a fishing vessel. And the girl went down to the shore every day, looking for him to come home. Of course, he never, never, NEVER came home. Ultimately she joined the ocean, hoping to float out and find him somewhere on the breast of the ocean.*

"I listen to the rush of the incoming tide." I remember singing this song as a kind of barcarole, ending with the girl wading into "the ocean sweet and wide."

JJN: The poet, of course, has got to be able to concentrate a whole life story into a very few sentences, and I think that's what we've been able to do here. Now we have the poetry of Thomas Merton, set to music by John Jacob Niles. This is an entire departure from anything we've done before, and in these numbers you will find the modernism that I've begun to love so much. This first one, Thomas called it "Carol"— I've called it "Nativity" because I felt the word "Carol" didn't carry that story sufficiently and he agreed with this. (We also have a daughter-in-law named Carol, and it became confusing). All right? "Flocks feed by darkness, with the noise, the noise of whispers, in the dry grass of pastures, and lull, the sound night lulled the night with their weak bells."

I knew this was an important moment, Johnnie's venture into a new kind of music. But it was also a Christmas party, with guests refreshing their drinks and chatting between songs, and oddly enough all that background activity and, yes, a certain level of inattention, relaxed me! Being surrounded with so many people didn't bother me at all: once we began, we were lost in the music— we had a wonderful time.

Singing in that room at Boot Hill was like magic. It's the greatest experience in the world for a singer to perform with the composer, in the room where the music was written. I always had a feeling for Johnnie's music at Boot Hill that was quite a challenge to capture on the concert stage.

JJN: Come in, honey, come in! [Rena says, "Elizabeth, why don't you just take this seat right there and then you won't have to go very far. We'll put Grace right next to Scotty."] Grace, sit right beside that red dress!

Now this is the second one in the series—"The Messenger"— it was meant to be the first, but somehow it has gravitated to the second position. It is more dissonant than the one before. "There is some sentry at the rim of winter."

This song has a flowing piano accompaniment, which Janelle played as a tender "romantic modernist" duet with the voice.

> *JJN: I suppose every creative artist in the world has had this experience. They say that as great a man as Monet would walk through the galleries and look at the pictures he had painted and say, "You know that's pretty good." And when I hear "The Messenger"— well, if I may boast a little bit, I think it's great stuff. Especially when you get all the notes in there.*

> *"The Responsory" is based on a kind of a sweeping melodic line— just play a moment or two of that— to me that is quite wonderful. I hope you will like it as well.*

I have always loved the difficult-to-sing words that begin this song: "Suppose the dead should crown their wit/ With some intemperate exercise." The guests warmed up to these songs as they heard more in the series. We finished the program with "The Flower of Jesse" and "Flame Within" which Johnnie introduced as usual.

> *JJN: As you all have discovered from the last few minutes, I am an Italian in many respects— I can run along very sweetly in a nice quiet way, but finally I conclude that the soprano has GOT to give us some results.*

The program concluded with an "Ave Maria" for cello and voice, with Johnnie's son John Ed on the cello. After a round of applause for this finale, everyone adjourned for a marvelous assortment of food— old ham, beaten biscuit, Mary Tippie Mullins'corn pudding— "a little bit of this, a little bit of that". Janelle and I met a number of Johnnie and Rena's friends, including Carolyn Hammer, the widow of Victor Hammer (who painted portraits of both Johnnie and Thomas Merton), and her nephew Gay Reading, who inherited the Victor Hammer Printing Press. I met Lorraine Windland, the woman who later painted my portrait,

Winnie Morriss, and Grace Webber, a lively and spirited woman who ran a prestigious private kindergarten in Lexington. Rena always had some of her friends from the Iroquois Hunt Club.

At any sort of gathering, but particularly one at her own home, Rena was the most delightful hostess, making everyone comfortable and happy. All who entered Boot Hill were required to sign her guest book in the vestibule next to the front door. But she had the most amazing social memory: at any time I could mention an event, and Rena was able to come up immediately with the names of people who were there. Rena had a real interest in people,

A rehearsal with Thomas Merton in preparation for the premier of the Niles-Merton songs
Photographer: Helm Roberts
Photo taken: 1968 ©

and she was unfailingly attentive. Someone said, "Rena Niles makes you feel like you're one of the most interesting people she has ever met." She would manage somehow to extend this warmth and charm to every single guest.

Johnnie's role as a magnanimous host was most closely associated with the music. He loved Christmas not only as an occasion for music but also because he was profoundly moved by the emotional and spiritual significance of the Blessed Mother and Child. Many of his songs are related to motherhood and indeed, several of the songs he chose for the performance that day were on that theme, from "Little Black Star" to the Niles-Merton songs to the final "Ave Maria."

I have always felt intuitively that many of Johnnie's songs expressed some of the tender or sorrowful or plaintive emotions that his public personality did not allow him to utter. One of these was a vast tenderness and deep devotion to his own mother. In his narratives, he talked a great deal about his father, yet in his music he so frequently is preoccupied with "mother." He treasured a carving of the Virgin and Child which he kept on his piano. I speculated, as I came to know Johnnie better, that the carving symbolized artistic creation as the blessing of a new birth. At a concert at Cortland College, he once referred to his love of this subject.

> JJN: *You just have got to be ready to accept miracles. That's what this is. For me, although I am inclined on the practical side, I love these kind of miracles. My wife said that I fell in love with the Blessed Mother when I was a very small boy or just a young man, and I have been writing love songs to her ever since. And there's a measure of truth in it; although I am not a Roman Catholic, I fell in love with the Blessed Mother.*

Though his public personality was well established and blended with his many aspects of his private personality, I also think that Johnnie was not comfortable speaking

about some things. Here his songs (and his poetry)
spoke for him.

Whatever the occasion, Rena was ever the diplomat, using
her grace and tact to smooth over any ruffled situation.
Johnnie could be outrageous and outspoken at times, but
Rena was always able to ease any stress caused by his
gruffness. It did not surprise me that their son Tom entered a career as a diplomat, while John Ed became a
director of an opera company. Johnnie and Rena worked
well as a team. Janelle and I were delighted to be asked to
join them in the Niles-Merton song project, yet we never
dreamed at that first Christmas party that we would
someday be invited to become a part of this team, to join
the "act."

We knew that Johnnie had performed alone for years,
depending only on Rena's able assistance. One day after
Janelle and I had become a part of the composing process
for the Niles-Merton song project and our visits to Boot
Hill Farm had become a happy twice- weekly routine,
Johnnie and Rena sat us down and told us suddenly that
they had been talking it over and they wanted to include
us in Johnnie's performances. This was an honor that we
were pleased to accept.

From then on, on stage and off, we were always referred to
as "the girls," which we thought did not describe us quite
accurately, since (as I have said before) we were mothers of
elementary school children. But Johnnie was in his seventies and eighties when Janelle and Nancie and I worked
with him, and because he relished what he could get away
with in his role as a clever old man, we let him tease us
and say outrageous things to us and to his audiences. We
just indulged him. By this time we were all good friends
and glad to be working together.

II

The Composing Process

Janelle and I shared a baby sitter for our children as we made the twice weekly trip out to Boot Hill. The routine was established that we would work from ten in the morning until noon. The drive from Lexington to the Niles farm was a pleasant one, and not too long: we would arrive and enter through the door on which Johnnie had hand-carved his dedication of this house— to the art of American song! While we worked at the piano, in the room where I had sung at Christmas, the carved statue of the Virgin and Child supervised our work.

Johnnie would have penciled in a newly composed part of a song on score paper, and we would sightread it for him. Then Johnnie would experiment with it, trying out variations and alterations. He described his creative process to a Newman Center audience.

> *JJN: I have my own way of composing. I sit quietly or lie in bed at night quietly with my arms at my sides and I say to myself, "I do not hate anything or anybody"— that's Zen. And I am at peace with the entire world. And if you say it over often enough and long enough, all*

kinds of magnificent ideas come crashing in on you. I
have pencil and paper and I write 'em down. Next
morning most of 'em are gibberish. I'm sorry. But I still
go on.

At last I had enough to do twenty-two songs, and the
twenty-two songs are done for Jackie Roberts. It took
about seven hundred and fifty pages of the very best
score paper I could possibly discover. Some of 'em were
six or eight pages long, and some of 'em were one page.
But I'm a terrific fellow for tearing up the music and
throwing it in the fireplace. I'm STILL throwing away
scraps of the first cycle.

When he was satisfied, he would compose a new section in
pencil, ready for our next session. He never copied out a
composition in ink until it was absolutely finished.
Johnnie would turn to us, at the end of a long period of
experimenting with various changes, and he would ask,
"What do you all think?" This signified that he was finally
fairly satisfied with what he had written. I usually replied,
"I think you've got something here, Johnnie."

JJN: And I couldn't be stopped for five years continuously.
I turned it out— I'm saying "I— I— I— I—," but I
don't know how else to tell the story. Then Jackie
came continually, trying, trying, trying, trying. If I
have any success with this enterprise, Tom Merton's
poetry, it'll be because Jackie encouraged me and was
willing to sing my strange cockeyed— attitudes, let
us say.

Johnnie had conceived these songs to be sung by a soprano, and as we worked on them, they were made to fit
my voice, which is actually a mezzo soprano. I think
Johnnie also appreciated being able to use my background
and training. He realized that he was writing art songs,
and he knew that this was some of the most complex
music he had ever attempted. He was also extremely
businesslike and particular about these compositions.

Our job was to be patient and to do our best for the material as he wrote it.

JJN: Jackie Roberts was able to take, learn, and sing the music. "Nativity" went through six entire versions before I arrived at the one offered.

Janelle was a marvellous sightreader, and she was very quick to pick up on the nuances that Johnnie would suggest to us. I think that some of the accompaniments, like the one for "Bird Cage Walk" were designed to show off Janelle's special capabilities and her precise yet fluid technique.

JJN: The girls called that one "The Cake Walk." It took me three months to finish.

At one recital in 1968, just after we'd performed "Love Winter When the Plant Says Nothing," Johnnie interrupted everything to draw attention to Janelle's accompaniment.

JJN: How about the tone quality in that run she did— isn't that beautiful? Do it for 'em again, honey. Let 'em hear it all over again. Just the run, just the run, yes.

Since the twenty-two Niles-Merton songs were written over a four year period, with our twice-weekly meetings going on in a fairly regular pattern, I think that Johnnie came more and more to trust us as good musicians. We could sight read and we could deliver the emotional quality that he wanted in his music. We were all totally absorbed in this fascinating project as Johnnie composed the songs. Johnnie once told an audience about the process of writing the beautiful song "Evening."

JJN: "Evening" is I think one of the most effective things we have. It's based on the whipporwill— play it, will you please, Janelle? We actually have whipporwills here, you know. People don't believe it, but we heard one in Lexington, Kentucky one night. It was so (sings the melody). They get started and wound up and you can't stop 'em somehow. It was at the home of the Hulls and

*we all went out in the back yard and it went on and on
and on and on. And I had the idea instantly like that. I
said, "Here's 'Evening' all right."*

*Here's an example, by the way. I'll tell you something about
the vagaries of composition. I had this thing written, and the
girls liked it, and we were working on it. And one day I
awoke in the middle of the night and said, "I'm mistaken!"
And I sat down here and went to writing it over, and I wrote
the central section of the melodic material over entirely and
gave it to the girls. They threw up their hands in holy horror
and said, "We won't sing it!" I went right back to the
original, and the original is right after all. You can't be sure
of yourself. You've got to have somebody about as smart as
this little girl here.*

Now for my two cents' worth. "Evening" was not a clear
manuscript, and I'd spent a good bit of time preparing the
first version. That is one reason I insisted he hear it. He
threw Version Two in the fire.

This was a hard-working and satisfying period. Janelle
and I were grateful that we were involved in something
that challenged us as musicians. As mothers of young
children, so much of our time was family-oriented: it
might have been tempting at this time to put the musical
side of our lives on hold. But twice a week we were
presented with new material and we had the opportunity
to participate as these beautiful songs emerged.

Johnnie was, I believe, challenging himself as well: he was
preoccupied with doing justice to Merton's poetry in a
musical form that was as contemporary as the ideas they
conveyed. He was exacting about the musical quality of
our performance, but when he was pleased he was generous with praise.

*JJN: When I was a very young man I encountered a
very great pianist in Paris, who taught me a great deal
about sound. He didn't make a pianist out of me because
I was just naturally not a pianist. But I have transferred
this idea to others I have worked with, particularly*

*accompanists, and this young woman has found out how
to produce that wonderful liquid quality in a fast passage
instead of just pounding out notes. You don't press both
notes down in an octave: you press one all the way down,
and the other one you just barely press down. And the one
you just barely press down produces an overtone, and there's
where that great French sound comes from.*

Paris was often in Johnnie's thoughts as he composed, as
were the great composers he had met. He spoke of Charles
Ives frequently. In a 1975 interview he gave to Noel
Coppage in *Stereo Review*, he told how Ives had urged him
at one point to try writing art songs. "Charles used to say
to me, 'Johnnie, why don't you give up this folklore nonsense?' He said, 'If you'll work with me, I can show you
how to put it together. You already have a good start,
you're very perceptive.'"

I know that Johnnie had a disarming way of making self-
deprecating remarks, just as he had his own way of boasting: since it was impossible to know exactly what transpired between him and Charles Ives, I just took what he
said at face value.

*JJN: When I was a very young fellow I came in contact
with one of the greatest composers ever to have lived in
the western world. His name was Charles Ives. It is my
considered judgment that Charles Ives will one day— of
course he's long dead— his music will finally become a
standard item in our catalogue. Already people model
composition on Charles Ives.*

*He was not accepted at the time I met him, and he had a
new vocabulary of curses for orchestral conductors. I had
been in the United States Army Air Corps, and at that time,
disabled out of the army, I understood all the words, I
thought. We used nearly all of them in the Air Corps
barracks. But Charles had some new ones. It didn't do him
any good— he knew it wouldn't— it didn't. He died
unwept, unhonored and unsung. But he left many disciples
behind him, among them Johnnie Niles.*

I know that Johnnie thought particularly of Charles Ives during the composing of "Ohio River." He nearly always referred to him when introducing that song, which to me has the American art song quality of Ives. But during this time Johnnie also cited Arnold Schoenberg as among his influences. I suspect that he was influenced by Schoenberg's words more directly than by his music, but I will let Johnnie tell it.

> *JJN: The thing that a great teacher of mine told me, he said, "You can write all the dissonance on earth. It has to be constructed dissonance and it has to resolve ultimately— even if it takes two weeks. Just wait around, and if it re- solves, the listeners will say 'Oh' and 'Ah.'" That was Arnold Schoenberg, and there never was another one like him.*

When Johnnie decided that a song was finished, he would often write a little personal note on the manuscript. Some- times these were simple— he would observe that he completed the song on the evening of the first frost of the season. Sometimes they were proud, as in the case of "Evening:" "this composition pleases me more than I can tell." Or he might describe his state of mind at the mo- ment. On "Wisdom" he noted, "I am so weary I could weep. This may be the last of it." (It wasn't: he wrote quite a few more songs after that). I treasure my working copies of these manuscripts for the flood of memories that they evoke of that creative period.

A typical working session lasted two hours. If the weather was chilly, there would be a big cheerful fire in the stone hearth. We were treated to a wonderful lunch. I've always been hungry after singing, but the meals that Mary Tippie Mullins prepared for us were very special. First, I remem- ber having a glass of wine or a Bloody Mary— in the coldest days of winter, my Bloody Mary would be served warm beside the fire. After that we would gather at the simple table on which Johnnie had carved the names of folk songs and ballads: Barbary Ellen, Black is the Color, I Wonder as I Wander, Little Mattie Groves.

Examples of Johnnie's woodcarving were to be seen everywhere, beginning as I mentioned with the beautiful front door of the house. In the large room where we rehearsed and performed in home recitals, there were several little carved birds. Johnnie loved birds. Maybe he felt an affinity to them because they too practiced the art of American song.

Once we had gathered at the dining table, with the wonderful fragrance of food from the kitchen pervading the room, Johnnie would ask the blessing. This was no perfunctory ritual: Johnnie's Grace was as substantial as the home-made bread he insisted upon.

> *JJN: Oh God, our heavenly Father, into Thy hands do we commit ourselves. Have mercy upon us, have mercy upon us, have mercy upon us. We thank Thee, oh God, for the food on this table, for the many hands engaged in the production of this food, from the fields to the kitchen and to the tables. Bless our cooks, bless the master and mistress of this house, and the guests within our gates. And give us the power, the willingness, the imagination, and the GUTS to go forward with whatever task is immediately before us. Into Thy hands do we commit ourselves, have mercy upon us, Amen.*

Quite often after Grace he would insist on reading a poem he had most recently written. He was working on the poems he published in *Brick Dust and Buttermilk* at the time. Sometimes as I listened to these poems I felt a little guilty that my appetite was dominating my love of art, as the scent of fresh warm bread and ham hinted of pleasures more basic than poetry. In their garden, Johnnie and Rena grew marvelous fresh vegetables and salad greens. Their asparagus bed was a particular point of pride. There is a video tape made of Johnnie during this period that shows him riding on his tractor while Rena works among the vegetables. Salads were a Niles favorite as well, and Johnnie's beloved fresh wholegrain bread— homemade, of course— appeared at almost every meal.

Mary Tippie Mullins was the kind of cook who seemed to bring out the true nature and flavor of the food. I know I was hungry, and as they say, "Hunger is the best sauce," but I also know that Mary Tippie had a genius for preparing food in such a way that the freshness of the ingredients were emphasized so beautifully that you thought you'd never eaten anything so fine in your life. Johnnie and Rena often carried their favorite special wholegrain bread with them when we toured.

I will always remember those luncheons with great satisfaction, but one particularly stands out, the day that Thomas Merton visited Boot Hill and we performed for him. There's a photograph taken of us around the piano. Johnnie is holding a paper in his hands and reading something to us that is making us all laugh. Thomas Merton has his hands on his hips and is looking at Johnnie with a sly amusement, and Janelle and I are just laughing out loud.

It was in October 1967 when Merton visited Niles and heard the first three songs Johnnie had written— "Messenger," "Carol," and "Responsory." It was a thrill for us to perform these songs for the poet who wrote them, and his response was so warm and enthusiastic. We had a wonderful lunch and I remember that Merton regaled us with hilarious stories: in particular, I recall his joking about the famous cheese produced at the monastery, Gethsemani.

I had never met Merton before that rehearsal. In fact, I had never even heard of him before we started work on the Niles-Merton songs. I thought I was going to meet a monk dressed in long dark robes, with a little cap on the back of his head. Instead, Merton arrived wearing jeans and heavy shoes that looked like the kind of steel-toed shoes that construction workers wear.

I sang the newly written songs from my heart. I was facing him while I sang. I will forever remember his expressions of joy and the tears in his eyes as he listened.

The second time he visited Boot Hill was the following year, when he heard seven of the songs we were preparing for a recital at Bellarmine College. On this occasion we performed "Sundown," "When You Point Your Finger," "The Lament of the Maiden," "The Weathercock on the Cathedral at Quito," "Love Winter When the Plant Says Nothing," and "Evening." Our Bellarmine College recital was scheduled for October 1968, but Merton had scheduled his fateful trip to Bangkok and would not be in the country.

After lunch we sat in a circle in the living room where Johnnie composed. Johnnie read some of his poetry and then Merton read his poetry for us. My husband Helm took a photograph, which I treasure, of us all listening to the poetry. Johnnie read him some of the *Brick Dust and Buttermilk* poems he had been regaling us with at lunch, and together they discussed some of the poems Johnnie had selected to include in the second "cycle," Opus 172: there were changes that Johnnie envisioned— a repetition here, a different word there, which he wanted to alter for the sake of the song. Merton encouraged him to go ahead and do so, saying, "You're the composer." Little did anyone realize how precious this conference time was, as Merton died during his trip abroad, but the Niles-Merton songs continued to pour out for several more years.

Johnnie's version of the way he came to the poetry of Thomas Merton was told to an audience at the Newman Center at the University of Kentucky.

> *JJN: As it worked out one day a man came to me—Victor Hammer the Viennese painter, and his wife Carolyn. They said to me, "Johnnie, you're wasting your time on a lot of nonsense. This poetry." I said, "My dear child, it's my poetry." "I know, but have you ever read Tom Merton's*

poetry?" I said, "I've read his book Seven Storey
Mountain." "All right, all right, here's the book, here's
the poetry— Selected Poems and the other one, Emblems
of a Season of Fury."

Carolyn Hammer has told me that Johnnie's account is
somewhat out of focus: her husband did not say that
Johnnie was wasting his time trying to write poetry—
that's just Johnnie's self-deprecating description. The
Hammers had been close friends with Merton for some
time, however, and had taken a good many picnics to
Gethsemani. Victor Hammer had painted the portraits of
both men and befriended them, so I'm sure that he was the
intermediary who introduced Johnnie to Merton's poetry.

*JJN: I sat down and looked at it. I was on the road a good
deal in those days singing music from here to Timbuctoo
and back. I carried one of those books with me and read it on
the road. I began to make notes in between the lines. That
book is going to be a collector's item of premier importance
some time, I think.*

In a 1971 concert at Agnes Scott College, Johnnie talked at
some length about Merton, his grief at his death, and the
philosophical territory that he felt he had in common with
the poet.

*JJN: One of the most rewarding experiences of my
long life— those of you who know how old I am, will
know what I mean when I say long life— was my
association with a Cistercian monk by the name of
Thomas Merton. He spent the first twenty-six years of
his life partly in France and some of it on Long Island
and some of it in New York City going to Columbia
University, ultimately teaching English, and finally
being converted to the Roman Catholic faith.*

*He began to write at a very early age, and the work for which
he is most widely known is The Seven Storey Mountain. I
hope you've all read it, and if you haven't, look up the
paperback copy and I think for around a dollar you'll have*

the vast experience of reading his autobiography. It is a biography up to that date, because he lived a long life after that.

Almost at once when he joined the Catholic Church he became a monk, and he came down to Kentucky and lived at the Gethsemani monastery a few miles from my home. I had the vast pleasure of having him there in my house— and my girls were there too at the same time. They had a great experience of it. We sang this music to him as it developed. From month to month, every week there was something new to show him and he sat on a bench across the room and wrung his hands over it.

I've already described the two visits Thomas Merton paid to Boot Hill: to me they were rare, priceless and far between. I think that Johnnie's account here, "from month to month, every week there was something new to show him" might have suggested to the Agnes Scott students a lot of visiting. But I realize now that Johnnie was composing with Merton constantly at his side— in his imagination. I'm sure he thought of each newly completed song as something to show Thomas. But getting permission to leave Gethsemani and plan visits to the outside world was not an easy matter, as I understand, which is why his friends so often traveled to visit him, instead of the other way around.

JJN: Thomas said, "John, I don't know if there is any such thing as existentialist music, but I believe that as my poetry is existentialist, your music is beginning to be." Well, that's a rather large statement!

I believe that this is an important observation: although I don't recall Merton saying this, it certainly describes how Johnnie realized that he was changing and growing as a composer, no longer writing "romantic modernism" but something totally new and relevant to the times.

JJN: I heard his magnificent poetry and "far-out" poetry, and realized I'd been missing something. And slowly the

music of the Niles-Merton cycle began to boil in my imagi-
nation. I also began to study Zen Buddhism. I studied Zen
diligently. I carry the book with me exactly as the little
Catholic priests carry their prayer book. It is the prayer book
for me. I looked at Thomas one day, and I said, "Thomas,
you are a Zen Christian, aren't you?" And he said, "I
congratulate you on your sense— your good sense— you
can see through things, can't you, Johnnie?" I said, "Well, I
hope I can. I hope I'm right this time." He said, "You're
right. I am a Zen Christian."

The fusion of poetry and music is one of the things I love
most, along with the challenge the singer faces in deliver-
ing this to an audience. Johnnie always insisted that I sing
from the heart. Sometimes during rehearsals, he would
weep openly, saying, "That's what I want! That's what I
want!" An intellectual understanding of the words was
never enough for Johnnie— he insisted upon a passionate
interpretation as well. It would be easy to say that his
years of performing ballads affected Johnnie's insistence
on passion, but that might be too simple. I could tell that
Merton's poetry moved him very deeply. And though
some of the poems were quite abstract and philosophical, I
learned from working with Johnnie how to find their
"heart" and convey it in performance.

A friend of mine pointed out that the ten songs of the first
"cycle" are all about being poised on the verge of change.
The anxiety and insecurities of the Cold War period
seemed to require a new perspective on spiritual matters,
which I believe Johnnie found first in his readings in Zen,
and then developed much more fully in his own way
through the Niles-Merton songs. I know it sounds odd to
factor "love" into all of this, but Johnnie rarely wrote about
anything else, and it was plain to me that he was express-
ing in some way the greatest love of his life.

The twelve songs of the second "cycle," it seems to me, are
filled with so many expressions of grief and sympathy and
love for Thomas Merton, Johnnie's slain partner.

JJN: If Tom had lived— and we regret his death so sorely— he'd be about fifty-six or seven years of age now. And of course he would only now be reaching a moment when the crescendo of his imagination would be functioning. I know I can tell you that in my case I was seventy-five before I got underway. But Thomas was a little bit better informed and smarter than I am.

In nearly every performance of these songs, Johnnie would make the point, "I am not a Roman Catholic." Usually he would go on from there to talk about Zen's influence on him.

JJN: I make bold to claim that I have the makings of a Zen in me. I'm pretty well Zen, I guess. He was too— that's the mystery of it all. Here was a Catholic who had embraced Zen Buddhism. That's what he was doing out there in Bangkok, visiting the monasteries of the various eastern faiths. I do not think we know positively how he died. It is generally accepted that he stepped on an electric line. Some how that doesn't stand up to me, knowing how strong that man was.

Even though he never said more than this publicly, Johnnie confided to close friends that he was very suspicious of the circumstances of Merton's death. I do know that he was particularly shaken by the news because he had had a premonition in a dream the very day of the death: "I saw Tom face down in water." He told me promptly about the dream, it bothered him so much. Newspaper reports came out a day or two later, telling of the fateful accident. Johnnie believed that Thomas had contacted him in this dream to let him know that he had been murdered.

Johnnie's grief was intense. Yet I could see that it gave him further stimulation to continue the process of composition postmortem— to do justice to the poems as well as his friend's memory in another dozen songs. Thomas Merton had been a catalyst in the creative transformation Johnnie was going through— and it always amazed him that it could be happening to him in his late seventies— and Johnnie persisted in the project. Zen and Merton had given him some insight into dealing with the disquiet and fear for humanity that this period brought with it. He found it necessary to share these insights through the songs.

I will never forget the evening in 1975 when we performed all twenty-two songs at the Newman Center at the University of Kentucky in Lexington. Father Moore had given a very kind introduction to the concert, saying, "The prime mover, of course, in this program is John Jacob Niles, who in his graciousness has asked that this first presentation of the full song cycles one and two of the poetry of Thomas Merton be done in a Roman Catholic Church. I would like to introduce to you John Jacob Niles." I dare say that Johnnie startled everyone there by the emphatic way he started his talk.

> *JJN: I am not a Roman Catholic. I'm— I might as well tell you the truth— I'm a Zen Buddhist. If the ceiling falls and hits me, it'll be all right. I think I can tell you that I spent quite a little time talking to Tom— this person right here (here he held up the book of Merton's poems) about Zen Buddhism. He was very well informed.*

In the course of this introduction, some of which I've quoted already, Johnnie surprised me by talking about me.

> *JJN: I came upon Jackie Roberts one day in my studio out at Boot Hill Farm. One Sunday afternoon she came in and I said, "Hello, who are you?" And she told me and she said, "I want to sing your music." Now that was a long while ago, seven years ago. I said, "All right, girl." And we began to work together.*
>
> *Jackie was able to take the music, learn the music, and sing the music. And we began singing a few pieces of it at a time, because I'm afraid, well— we were faint-hearted, we weren't sure yet. Finally someone of authority came along and said,*

"Why you've got something here." We said, "Have we?" And that was it.

And then Father Moore came and said, "Let's do it all at once!"

"Well," I said, "Father, it's a mixture of religions. I'm— well, you know what I am, nothing perhaps, maybe Zen Buddhist, and my sweet girl is certainly not a Roman Catholic."

And he said, "Oh forget about that foolishness." So here we are tonight. And it gives me great pleasure to tell you that we're going to try to do all twenty-two of the songs.

Now sit quietly, study what you hear. Don't expect too much. In that way, you'll get more than if you start out to expect a lot and then don't get anything— do you know what I mean?

*Concert at Transylvania University
Photographer: Helm Roberts
Photo taken: 1975 ©*

III

Poetry and Song: Opus 171

I will tell more about the Newman Center recital, when we performed all twenty-two of the Niles-Merton songs, a little later, because I want to return to the poetry and philosophy of those songs. I think you can truly say that the composer revered the Merton poetry, because he insisted that the musical performance carry that reverence for the words. Johnnie preferred to give an audience a program with the text of the poems. If that was not possible, he (or after his death Rena) would simply read the poem about to be sung.

> *JJN: Do not expect to understand all the texts at once.*
> *Take those texts home with you. They're valuable.*
> *Read 'em carefully, prayerfully. Get yourself a volume*
> *of the introduction to Zen by Suzuki. You can buy it*
> *for seventy-five cents to a dollar in any bookstore— it's*
> *a paperbound book. And read it! And study it!*

He would emphasize the importance of listening in a receptive contemplative state, and he advised audiences that understanding would come slowly. He explained his own experience with the Merton poetry at Agnes Scott College in 1971.

> *JJN: I do not expect you to understand the philosophy and the meaning behind these words at first glance. Prima facie you do not understand existentialist poetry. At least not this.*
>
> *I am not thought to be the stupidest man in Boone Creek Valley in Kentucky— and I tell you I didn't get it. It took me some time. It wasn't until it was well set to music that the meaning of the thing began to percolate to me. And it showed me something about how important it is that poetry should be set to music if you ever expect to understand it completely.*

Actually Johnnie's whole career was firmly based on the interrelationship of music and poetry, though here I think he was thinking of Merton's poetry as being in a separate— perhaps a philosophical— category. In any case, he was a little reluctant to analyze the poetry in his prefatory remarks. He would talk freely about how the music came to him, or he would comment on the background of the song. But always he would make the point about religion.

> *JJN: I remarked to the young ladies from Bellarmine that a collection of godforsaken Protestants were doing pretty well by the Catholic Church. As we said, it was an ecumenical effort of the first order. We're all Protestants except Mr. Merton.*

Only eight of the poems, "The Messenger," "Nativity," "Sundown," "Evening," "For My Brother," "Cana," "Jesus Weeps Into the Fire" and "Mosaic" make specific reference to Christianity, yet to me all of the songs have spiritual power. There are meditations on nature and on silence. There are two elegies, "Lament of the Maiden for the Warrior's Death" and "For My Brother Reported Missing in Action, 1943." Certainly Merton's social concern over the Cold War informs "A Responsory, 1948," and the threat of racial violence underlies "The Ohio River— Louisville." And "The Greek Women" and "The Weathercock of the Cathedral of Quito" are very dramatic. But quite aside from classification, I love them all.

Let me take the songs in the order in which they are presented in The Niles-Merton Songs, and share some of my thoughts and Johnnie's comments on each one. It is only in the last stanza of "The Messenger" that you realize that it is about the Annunciation: but the three stanzas preceding are about March, "at the rim of winter" preparing for "the coming of the warrior sun." This is an energetic song, not only because of the words but because of the suggestion of an armed camp awaiting war.

> *There is some sentry at the rim of winter*
> *Fed with the speech the wind makes*
> *In the grand belfries of the sleepless timber. . .*
> *When Gabriel hit the bright shore of the world,*
> *Yours were the eyes saw some*
> *Star-sandalled stranger walk like lightning down the air*
> *The morning that the Mother of God loved and dreaded*
> *the message of an angel.*

This is the song that Johnnie bragged on at the Boot Hill Christmas party, "When I hear 'The Messenger'— well, if I may boast a little bit, I think it's great stuff. Especially when you get all the notes in there." (I was pretty sure we'd gotten all the notes in there!)

Johnnie would explain that he'd changed the title of Merton's poem "Carol." Sometimes he would say that he didn't think of the poem as a carol, and at other times he would say that because his daughter-in-law's name was Carol, things just got too confusing. I always thought the former was the real reason.

JJN: The demands of the music, you know, make it necessary for me to leave out words and put in words. He [Merton] said, "You're writing the music— I only know poetry." So when the time came we renamed this thing. I named it "The Nativity." He said, "Let's name it "Nativity." Now of all the material, this is the first one to have been accepted by the publishers. And I just read the proof on it for a chorus of women's voices and a mixed chorus SATB [soprano, alto, tenor, bass]. I suppose you'll see it published in about a year.

One would think that Thomas Merton would write quite often about the birth of Christ, the Nativity. But in all of the poems we have, I find only one concerning the Nativity. 'Flocks feed by darkness with a noise, a noise of whispers.' They produced a lot of milk, they still produce a lot of milk at Gethsemani, and he knows all about milking machines and early morning operations in the cow barn.

In later performances we often began a selection of these songs with "A Responsory," Merton's Cold War paradox. This is a wonderful opening song for a program, and I think that it prepares the audience nicely for the special quality of these songs.

JJN: Here we have "The Responsory." It's the only ballad form Thomas Merton went into. There is a refrain, as you see in the text, repeated three times.

> *Suppose the dead could crown their wit*
> *With some intemperate exercise,*
> *Spring wine from their ivory*
> *Or roses from their eyes. . .*
> *Two cities sailed together*
> *For many thousand years*
> *And now they drift asunder.*
> *The tides of new wars*
> *Sweep the sad heavens,*

Divide the massed stars,
The black and white universe
The booming of the spheres. . .

JJN: There's one place in here that is a little bit difficult for me to understand, and I didn't have time to corner Thomas with it. "Two cities sailed together for a thousand years, now they drift asunder." I'll see him next Saturday morning and I'm going to corner him first thing.

My understanding was that the two cities— and the black and white universe— referred to the superpowers and the ways in which their armed standoff created a world of suffering and separation, a limbo-like place. I like the riddling quality of "the dead are not yet dead/ And the living live apart."

JJN: "The Responsory"... is concerned with great sweeps of sound and has a considerably complicated accompaniment.

"Sundown," translated by Merton from the Spanish of the Nicaraguan poet Alfonso Cortes, is a serenade. Johnnie's note on the manuscript requests that the piano accompaniment be played "as if on muted strings." For all of its sweetness melodically, it is brooding and a little frightening in its subject.

. . . O sundown,
The hour, sad in time, calls back to life the strong
Sight of Bethlehem:
The hound of night bays in this sky of a long
Time ago,
And down to the horizon goes
A troop of unknown bodies and shadows.

JJN: "Sundown" is in Emblems of a Season of Fury. *It is a translation of a poem written by Alfonso Cortes, a*

Central American poet, who has spent quite a lot of his life
in an insane hospital. When he's in the hospital and he's
confined and restrained, he writes the best poetry. And
when he is sane and out in the great world, his poetry is dull
and definitely uninteresting.

I had to sing "horizon" with the emphasis on the first
syllable, and I was always grateful when Johnnie would
read the poem through first, pronouncing it that way.

*JJN: I think Cortes has done one of the great love poems of
all time— Jackie will sing it in a few moments, called "When
You Point Your Finger." This is a very Zen poem. We have
the transcript— isn't that sweet? "If someone asks you your
origin/ Say it is from Him you come." This is a very Zen
statement, turning everything inward toward yourself. This
man says, "On the day you love, love will be made over into
something new." I tell you those Central Americans have
something you have to consider there. They understand a lot
of things we never found out about. Particularly this one,
who is utterly insane.*

There's another story about the "tune," as Johnnie called it,
written for this song: I'll pass on that story in another
chapter on our concertizing and touring. Suffice it to say
that Johnnie had composed some of the music for this song
years earlier, and for various reasons it did not become
part of the repertoire, so he "recycled" it.

When you point your finger

Oblivion stops, surprised,

And if you call

The Future turns around and lies at your feet. . .

If someone asks your origin, say

It is from Him you come.

To those who do not know your way

Answer, you go toward Thyself.

Another translation— there are five of them in Opus 171—
is "The Weathercock on the Cathedral of Quito." Merton
translated the poem from the Spanish of Jorge Carrera
Andrade. This is quite a change of pace from the meditations above: this is fun, dramatic, romantic and even a
little bit sexy. It tells of a weathercock who has fallen
in love with a seductive and beautiful lady named Anna
del Campo.

> JJN: Here's another one that has these wonderful Zen
> suggestions in it. The poem, as aesthetic as it is, concerns
> this "tin Don Juan," the weathercock. And he is "paralyzed
> in a desert of roofs"— a "cathedral ascetic." Isn't that
> sweet? Anna del Campo passes by, and he flashes signals to
> his friend the lightning rod. The idea of including the word
> "lightning rod" in a poem that is to be set to music was a
> complete shock and surprise to me. But I took it in the Zen
> way, and I'm delighted to think that I've been so successful
> with it.

> Silver cock, in the wind,
>
> Silver cock, paralyzed
>
> In a desert of roofs.
>
> Cathedral ascetic,
>
> He knows no other corn
>
> Than the sky's kind: hail.
>
> As Anna del Campo goes by,
>
> He flashes sun signals
>
> To his friend the lightning rod.

> JJN: The weathercock is made of metal and cannot
> have any friends of the other sex. There aren't any
> female weathercocks, apparently, and there he stands
> on top of this cathedral— "poor tin Don Juan."

Scottish slipper chair and "B" dulcimer
John Jacob Niles-signed and dated
Size: 3.75 x 4.75
Photo taken: 1934 ©

I enjoy dramatizing both characters. "Anna del Campo" introduces a sultry passage in the midst of the poor rooster's desperation. The accompaniment is a kind of leisurely march, as the lady saunters in the street below.

> JJN: *Almost in the tradition of the medieval priests, Thomas Merton translates and encourages the use of the love poem— "Anna del Campo passes by."*

At Agnes Scott College, when introducing this song, Johnnie startled everyone with his remarks.

> JJN: *"The Weathercock On the Top of the Cathedral at Quito" is as near a love song, I suppose, as Thomas ever got. It is said he had a wife in London at one time in his life. I'm not sure of that. He didn't talk about it.*

Next in the series of songs is "Evening," which Johnnie based on the song of the whipporwill.

> JJN: *You all recognize the whipporwill's call— do you all have whipporwill up in this country? Well, we have many of them down there in Kentucky, and I have counted thirty-five "whipporwills" from one bird at one time before he stopped to get his breath. He's a fabulous singer. Has no variations, he only says one thing, but he says it magnificently.*

> They say the sky is made of glass
>
> They say the smiling moon's a bride.
>
> They say they love the orchards and the appletrees,
>
> The trees, their innocent sisters, dressed in blossoms,
>
> Still wearing, in the blurring dusk,
>
> White dresses from that morning's first communion.
>
> And, where blue heaven's fading fire last shines,
>
> They name the new come planets
>
> With words that flower
>
> On little voices, light as stems of lilies.
>
> And, where blue heaven's fading fire last shines,

Reflected in the poplar's ripple,

One little, wakeful bird

Sings like a shower.

I heard Sister Therese Lentfoehr, the author of *Words and Silence*, speak of this poem, developing the reference to the innocence of children taking their first communion. Johnnie noted on the manuscript when he completed it, "This pleases me more than I can tell."

JJN: "One little wakeful bird sings like a shower." This breaks me up completely.

I have always loved "little voices, light as stems of lilies—" the words and the music seem to be trading roles. The whipporwill call just becomes softer and softer until it stops.

JJN: The whipporwill's call is in every measure.

The next song, "Great Prayer," is very brief and very demanding to sing because of the way the vocal line breaks.

JJN: This number is called "Great Prayer" in the book of poetry, but we have merely called it "Prayer." As we rehearsed this music, the girls made all the titles over. This poem was written by Alfonzo Cortes and translated by Thomas Merton.

Time is hunger, space is cold

Pray, pray, for prayer alone can quiet

The anxieties of void.

Dream is a solitary rock

Where the soul's hawk nests:

Dream, dream, during

Ordinary life.

JJN: As I told you people, it is rather hopeless to try to understand this poetry the first time around. "A Great Prayer," for example. "Dream is a solitary rock where the soul's hawk nests."

Have you noticed the number of birds that are mentioned in these songs? They remind me of the little woodcarvings that Johnnie had made and kept in Boot Hill. Birds certainly inspired him— eight of the songs feature birds in some way. They had practiced the art of song from the very beginning, I suppose. Johnnie talked often of walking in the woods, listening to the birds, when he was composing music or poetry. The next song, "Love Winter When the Plant Says Nothing" is a meditation upon nature.

> *O little forests, meekly*
>
> *Touch the snow with low branches!*
>
> *O covered stones*
>
> *Hide the house of growth!*
>
> *Secret*
>
> *Vegetal words*
>
> *Unlettered water,*
>
> *Daily zero. . .*
>
> *Oh peace, bless this mad place:*
>
> *Silence, love this growth.*
>
> *Oh silence, golden zero,*
>
> *Unsetting sun.*
>
> *Love winter when the plant says nothing.*

JJN: Do not be surprised at the text. We find lines— "daily zero"— "unlettered water"— "pray undisturbed"— "curled tree"— "carved in steel"— "fire turneth inward." It has to do with the Zen process of looking down into yourself.

Now the idea of introducing that sentence— "oh secret vegetal words"— how are you going to set it to music and make it convincing? I think we did.

The song must lead up to "bless," a sustained high G, and then quietly settle into "nothing." I think of this and some of the other Zen songs as being very spare and lean, pared down to the essentials of word and sound.

JJN: All right. "Love Winter When the Plant Says Nothing." I went to a performance this last winter at the Coliseum. You know, Coliseum performances bore me to extinction, but this one was a little less boring than the others. There was a chorus of some kind of— I thought they were Mexicans or some kind of South Americans— and they got ahold of a song where everything was on a monotone. And it was very, very effective— it has influenced me enormously. I've used this, you see, this afternoon. I used it in "Evening" and I use it again here, in this one. It proves to me that you don't need a great many notes. We use a great many, I think, without really many times realizing we don't need 'em at all— we're just bolstering up our inability to create something with a few notes. Like painting with a few colors.

Now. "Lament of the Maiden for the Warrior's Death." I suppose you must know that most of our melodic conventions here are based on Gregorian modes. Almost every one. Might as well be over here at Gethsemani.

> *. . .Ever since the old days*
>
> *Death has stalked*
>
> *And yet*
>
> *Your silence is new,*
>
> *And new is my pain!*

Without the title, the dramatic elements in the song would be more generic: as it is, it too is quiet and spare, a meditation and an elegy. When I review them now, the songs in Opus 171 are intensely reflective and even apprehensive— facing the "anxieties of void." At the time they were composed there was, as there is now, a sense that the country's spiritual compass had been lost or at least misplaced. Death and dread seemed all the more horrible in a world that seemed unable to give life some meaning.

The Second World War, Korea, and Vietnam were all imprinted on Thomas Merton's consciousness and fixed in his grief. The many calls to prayer— "pray undistracted" and "prayer alone can quiet/ The anxieties of void" seemed to me to come from Merton's spiritual discipline— I know that he instructed the young monks at Gethsemani in these matters. Johnnie's own discovery of Zen Buddhism at the time was a point of mutual understanding. Each man had his own history— very different from the other's. But there can be no question of their shared sympathies, or that John Jacob Niles, in Opus 171, captured the anxiety of the times, understood the struggle with emptiness, and ultimately arrived at a kind of meditative acceptance of it. In this context he found the music for these poems.

IV

The Twelve Songs of Opus 172

The twelve songs that were written after Thomas Merton's death seem to me to have some different qualities from the first ten songs, even though the first four songs in this new opus are transitional in that they are meditative and reflect the influence of Zen. The first of the series, "O Sweet Irrational Worship," Johnnie dedicated to me. It serves as a kind of bridge between the two sets of songs. Thomas Merton never heard these songs, and never knew of their existence, yet I know in my heart that Johnnie believed that somehow the music would cross freely to the afterlife.

> *I am earth, earth*
>
> *My heart's love*
> *Bursts with hay and flowers. . .*
>
> *I am earth, earth.*
>
> *Out of my grass heart*
> *Rises the bobwhite.*
>
> *Out of my nameless weeds*
> *His foolish worship.*

I can only suppose that Merton was in Johnnie's thoughts, for this certainly seems like a meditation on the survival of the soul. The bobwhite's call runs through this song, just as the whipporwill runs through "Evening."

When Johnnie and Rena traveled abroad in 1972, they sent me a postcard. All it said, in Johnnie's handwriting was, "Sing, sweet bird/ I hear your trills." This song and "Autumn," the next one, focus on birds. "Autumn" is translated from the French of Raissa Maritain: in it a sparrow's tears turn to glass on a cold branch.

> . . .*The bird wept by itself*
> *Flowering the dark elm*
> *With tears in blossoms*
> *Of glass and new gold*
> *Both branch and sparrow*
> *In mist grey and pure*
> *Marry their homesickness*
> *With the night's mystery.*

On my copy of the manuscript, Johnnie had noted, drawing two arrows to point out the two minor chords that end the piece, "This is the mystery."

The next two songs are Zen, to my way of thinking. "Wisdom" is full of paradox and humor, with the same kind of wit that is in "Responsory." Let go of your search for wisdom and knowledge, it seems to say.

> *I studied it and it taught me nothing.*
> *I learned it and soon forgot everything else:*
> *Having forgotten, I was burdened with knowledge—*
> *The insupportable knowledge of nothing.*

How sweet my life would be, if I were wise!

Wisdom is well known

When it is no longer seen or thought of.

Only then is understanding bearable.

On my copy of the manuscript, Johnnie repeats "or thought of" and notes that it must be sung as an after-thought ("prolong: an afterthought") so that it seems as if the singer is realizing one more thing in the very course of the song. When he finished writing this song, he noted on the manuscript, "I am so weary I could weep. This may be the last of it." In fact, "the insupportable knowledge of nothing" seems to be a theme that Johnnie loved in Thomas Merton's poetry. And in "The Mirror's Mission," a translation of Jorge Carrera Andrade's poem, there is also an idea of absence and silence.

JJN: In Zen Buddhism we say, "He who knows does not speak and he who speaks does not know."

...You make the shadows yield to your bright will.

Your mineral silence glows in the dark.

...Each chair opens out, waits in the night

To seat some unreal guest before a dish of shadows.

You alone, transparent witness,

Recite your lesson learned by heart— your lesson

of light.

On my copy of the manuscript, Johnnie had written, "Where have I been all this time to have missed such fabulous ideas?'

"Elegy: For My Brother Reported Missing in Action, 1943" is the song which, from the time it was written, we almost always included in my performance of the Niles-Merton songs. Johnnie completed it after Thomas Merton's death, and it is a perfect expression of the range of grief from desolation and despair to anger and, finally, a prayerful resolution.

JJN: Thomas Merton's brother went to France in the Second World War and never came back. They never found his body. He, again, was fighting a war to end all wars. As you may imagine, Thomas is rather definite on the subject of warfare. He was violently opposed to war. His poem "For My Brother" is really a device to pour out his heart over this sorrow and suffering that the death of his loved one caused. (Pause). They never found his body.

I can never sing this without thinking of Merton himself, killed in a faraway place, and the brotherly feelings that Johnnie himself had developed for the poet. The songs written thus far in Opus 172 have all been in one way or another concerned with grief, absence, and the afterlife. But "For My Brother" is the fullest, most expressive and most formal— poetically as well as musically— elegy.

Elegy: For My Brother
Reported Missing in Action, 1943

Sweet brother, if I do not sleep

My eyes are flowers for your tomb;

And if I cannot eat my bread,

My fasts shall live like willows where you died.

In the heat I find no water for my thirst,

My thirst shall turn to springs for you, poor traveller.

Where, in what desolate and smokey country,

Lies your poor body, lost and dead?

. . .For in the wreckage of your April Christ lies slain

And Christ weeps in the ruin of my spring;
The money of Whose tears shall fall
Into your weak and friendless hand,
And buy you back to your own land:

The silence of Whose tears shall fall
Like bells upon your alien tomb.
Hear them and come: they call you home.

JJN: Many years before, I had been concertizing in Holland, and I saw eight men carrying a coffin on their shoulders. Peasants they were, and they wore tall black hats— black clothes— slogging through the December mud. Somehow, although there was no music actually being played, I heard music. And I wrote it down and kept it many's the year. Ultimately it found its place in this composition. You will find the funeral march runs all the way through the piece, and comes finally to the end, which is definitely the expression of the funeral march.

This is a song which invariably moves the audience: the emotion is deeply embedded in the words and music, and there is progressive movement throughout from grief to tenderness to rage and on toward the Christian resolution. But it adds up to more than just a sum of its parts: this song has a spiritual power which is greater than just the words or just the music. There is often a contemplative, breath-catching hush in the audience before they begin to react.

"The Greek Women" is a dramatic song that I like to include for academic audiences who know the story of Agamemnon. The song presents a picture of the stylish women awaiting the warrior's return. "Beads and brace-lets gently knifeclash all about her"— this is quite a challenge to my diction, as you may imagine, and that "knife" has to stand out to create the sense of menace.

The ladies in red capes and golden bracelets
Walk like reeds and talk like rivers,
And sigh, like Vichy water, in the doorways. . .

JJN: *I said to Thomas, "Vichy water?" He said, "I suppose
you've pressed on the little lever on a bottle of Vichy water
and heard it fizz?" I said, "Yes," and he said, "Well, that
was what the women were doing, they were fizzing." He
was not overly impressed, you see.*

All spine and sandal stand the willow women;
They shake their silver bangles
In the olive-light of clouds and windows,
Talking, among themselves, like violins. . .

All your men are sleeping in the alien earth,
But one.
And Clytemnestra, walking like a willow, stares.
Beads and bracelets gently knifeclash all about her,
Because the conqueror, the homecome hero,
The soldier Agamemnon
Bleeds in her conscience, twisting like a root.

JJN: *Father Merton's interest in the history of the Greeks
and my fascination with Eric Satie led us finally to the
composition of "The Greek Women." I took Thomas to task
for the use of the word "violins" in the same sentence
practically with "Clytemnestra." He said, "Oh, don't be
tiresome." The violin was a development many, many
centuries later—Stradivari, in Pomona, Italy. I said,
"Thomas, no!" But he was fascinated with the word
"violin," not necessarily the music. That's how it got into
the poem, I'm sure.*

Violins reappear in "Cana," one of the autobiographical

poems about Merton's experience as a young monk. Johnnie wrote this during his mourning period for his friend, when he was working through an understanding of his life in order to deal with his untimely death.

Once when our eyes were clean as noon, our rooms
Filled with the joys of Cana's feast:
For Jesus came, and His disciples, and His Mother,
And after them the singers
And some men with violins. . .

We saw our earthen vessels, waiting empty.
What wine those humble waterjars foretell!
Wine for the ones who, bended to the dirty earth,
Have feared, since lovely Eden, the sun's fire,
Yet hardly mumble, in their dusty mouths, one prayer.

Wine for old Adam, digging in the briars!

I remember Johnnie saying, when Janelle struck the lowest possible D octave at the end of this song, "That's me! I am old Adam!" On my copy of the original manuscript, Johnnie had abandoned the formal authorship he usually wrote at the top of the page, and substituted simply "Thomas" and "John." The song itself is a sweet tribute to the young and hopeful monks.

In contrast, "Ohio River" is a warning about the young and the hopeless. This song is always popular with Kentucky audiences, and I sometimes wonder if they completely understand what Merton was saying about violence in our society.

No one can hear the loud voice of the city
Because of the tremendous silence
Of this slow-moving river, quiet as space.

Not the towering bridge, the crawling train,
Not the knives of pylons
Clashing in the sun...

All life is quieter than the weeds
On which lies lightly sprawling,
Like white birds shot to death,
The bathers' clothing.

But only where the swimmers float like alligators,
And with their eyes as dark as creosote
Scrutinize the murderous heat,
Only there is anything heard:
The thin, salt voice of violence,
That whines, like a mosquito, in their simmering blood.

One of the interesting things about this song is its lullaby-like quality, a kind of soothing rhythm that contrasts with the harshness of the industrial imagery.

*JJN: Charles Ives came to me one day and said, "Now this is what you want to use, boy. Give up that right-hand business of using all your fingers in the right hand. Just take this board— it's got a piece of felt on the bottom of it, and jam it down on all the black keys every now and then, and then you've got a lot of music." Well, I got ahold of a board and tried it and I wasn't ready for it, you see— I was only a Boone Creek boy in the great world— I did my best. And Charles died and I went on with folk music. But when I got around to these compositions, I realized that it was time for me to listen to someone as great as Charles Ives. I gave the board to Nancie, [*Nancie Field, my accompanist at this time*] and I wrote this piece based on a poem of Thomas Merton's entitled "Ohio River."*

I will never forget how Johnnie took me by surprise one day. Right after he made these remarks about Charles Ives and the board we used in this song, he went on.

> *JJN: It is interesting to say that this little girl over there sitting at the piano was born in a hollow just above the Ohio River. She's right off the mountainside. She knows all about the Ohio River. As far as the river is concerned, it was booming past her all her early days.*

Right off the mountainside! Where did he get that? I was from Russell, Kentucky, true enough: but I could hardly control my expression as I sat there trying not to look like the wild woman he seemed to be describing in his introduction.

Thomas Merton could be quite funny and slightly scathing about some of the pseudoholidays this country celebrates, like "National Pickle Week." Father's Day was one of these, to his way of thinking. In "Original Sin," he plays with this idea by honoring an imagined Neanderthal father who pounds crudely on words with a big bone. He called this poem "A Memorial Anthem for Father's Day."

> *Weep, weep, little day*
> *For the Father of the lame*
> *Experts are looking*
> *For his name*
>
> *Weep, weep, little day*
> *For your Father's bone*
> *All the expeditions*
> *Dig him one.*
>
> *. . .Weep, weep little day*
> *For his walking and talking*
> *He walked on two syllables*
> *Or maybe none*

Weep little history
For the words he offended

One by one
Beating them grievously
With a shin bone.

Johnnie picked right up on the title's suggestion of an anthem: this song opens with a swaggering waltz-time introduction, and it winds up with two funny little whimpers— "Ah! ah!"— as if in response to the beating. It is a witty piece of music for a witty poem.

The next song, "Birdcage Walk," is one of the poems Johnnie had discussed at length with Thomas Merton. It is somewhat fable-like, like many of his poems written in the late fifties. It comes from the collection called *The Strange Islands*, and it is based on a childhood memory.

> JJN: *Thomas said rather reluctantly that this poem might have been named "The Palace Girls." Some of Thomas Merton's admirers will object to this but I think I know quite well what he was trying to say. It is in fact autobiographical with Thomas being the Bishop.*

> *. . .Then*
> *Come cages made of pretty willows*
> *Where they put the palace girls!*

> *. . .Chinese fowl fought the frosty water*
> *Startled by this old pontifex.*

> *"No bridge" (He smiled*
> *Between the budding branches),*
> *No crossing to the cage*
> *Of the paradise bird!"*

Astounded by the sermons in the leaves
I cried, "No! No! The stars have higher houses!"

That was the bold day when
Moved by the unexpected summons
I opened all the palace aviaries
As by a king's representative
I was appointed fowler.

I think Johnnie was particularly interested in the indirect way the subject of celibacy was addressed in this poem. The rebellion of the boy, freeing the caged girls and breaking the rule of the bishop, appealed to him. Johnnie wrote a lavish accompaniment which was inspired by the chance to show off Janelle's fine technique.

    JJN: My girls call this "Cake Walk."

"Jesus Weeps Into the Fire" is the title Johnnie gave the next song, which was titled only as "80" in *Cables to the Ace*, although Merton described it in his notes as the "slowly hymn."

Slowly slowly
Comes Christ through the garden
Speaking to the sacred trees. . .

Slowly slowly
Comes Christ through the ruins
Seeking the lost disciple
A timid one
Too literate
To believe words
So he hides

Slowly slowly
Christ rises on the cornfields
It is only the harvest moon. . .

The disciple will awaken
When he knows history
But slowly slowly
The Lord of History
Weeps into the fire.

Johnnie added a third "slowly" for emphasis to the opening line.

This poem may or may not be autobiographical, with Merton empathizing with the doubting disciple as much as with Jesus' grief. I understand that one of the reasons Johnnie selected this poem was for its allusion to Gethsemani, the garden where Christ was arrested and accused, the place of great suffering. But Gethsemani is also the name of the Kentucky monastery where Merton had spent so much of his life and where he now had retired into his "hermitage" or separate dwelling on the property. Surrounded by cornfields and gardens, Merton wrote many articles on social issues and nuclear war in this place, as well as essays on the subject of monastic discipline. Johnnie and Rena had been to visit him there several times, bringing picnic lunches. The doubleness of the reference appealed to Johnnie.

"Mosaic" is the last of the songs. In 1970, Johnnie had finished twenty-one songs, but he was oddly superstitious about numbers. He told us once that the number twenty-two had particular significance for him, or so he had been told by a numerologist, and he was uneasy until he achieved that number of songs.

"Mosaic" is a translation from the French of Raissa Maritain. It is a poem honoring the Virgin Mary as well as "love art and poetry," so it offers a closure, or resolution, to the series.

> *So like a quiet pigeon in a hollowed rock*
> *You stand there in the wall's curve*
> *Made of stone needled tapestry*
> *In this dim sheltered paradise*
> *Mary made of love art and poetry*

I'm pretty sure that Johnnie liked the pigeon simile in this song too, because the Niles-Merton songs are full of bird images— the bobwhite, the whipporwill, the weathercock, the "little wakeful bird," ducks and swans and "paradise birds," as well as "white birds shot to death." The song-bird and the composer have a common effect, I suppose, at times— detaching the listener briefly from ordinary thoughts and lightly lifting the mind out of itself and taking it to a different place.

These songs have a powerful effect: I have been singing them for the last twenty-odd years, and they never fail. Whether people remember John Jacob Niles or Thomas Merton or not, the songs invariably move audiances and transform them in some way. On my manuscript copy of "Mosaic," Johnnie wrote a kind of formal postscript.

> *JJN: I started these two cycles, Opus 171 and 172, with*
> *"The Messenger" 3 years ago, and though it ws the most*
> *moving musical and creative experience of my entire life,*
> *many times I have wished I had never heard tell of this*
> *wonderful "Poetic" material. It taught me a new kind of*
> *music composition and the writing of poetry.*

He signed this "Johnnie Niles." Then beneath this he wrote, as an aftertought:

> *JJN: P.S. For me nothing has ever been the same.*

V

On Stage — The Storyteller

Johnnie asked me to be a part of his seventy-seventh
birthday performance in 1969. This was to be held at the
Cincinnati Conservatory, which was his alma mater.
Johnnie viewed his birthday as something of a state occasion. He always scheduled a birthday concert to present
the world with his most recent music and to celebrate the
triumphant survival of another year in his long and fruit-
ful life.

He and Janelle and I had carefully prepared for this concert, warming up for it you might say, by giving two
concerts in the previous months, one at Bellarmine College
in Louisville and one at the University of Kentucky. At
Bellarmine, we had been part of their Town and Gown
week, an annual event honoring education. I remember
that Thruston Morton was one of the speakers. Our
concert was held on a Sunday, the last day of the week-
long event. We performed in Knight's Hall, which was a
gymnasium, really. It had a very high ceiling and was
complete with basketball hoops. There was no amplification available in the gym, and big double service doors
opened to the outside. I remember waiting through the
first part of the program backstage in an area that was

unheated, and wishing that I'd brought a sweater. But the place was full of people who appreciated the new music.

The reviewer, Jean Dietrich, wrote the next day, "The joint work of John Jacob Niles and Thomas Merton is an inspired collaboration." This concert "gave a spiritual dimension to the series of secular activities known as Town and Gown Week." At the other warm-up concert, in Memorial Hall at the University of Kentucky, Johnnie talked a great deal about his inspiration for the Niles-Merton music and then changed tone a little bit and told other stories about the sources of his more familiar pieces. I remember that at the end of this concert he took the audience into his confidence, making them feel that they were the only ones he ever told these stories to.

> *JJN: Well, ladies and gentlemen, I think you've had it. In performance, I promise you, I'm not going to be giving out all this interlinear conversation. I simply can't do it, because I think it would disturb the house too much. From now on, when someone says to me, "How about seeing your script?" Script? I haven't got a script!*

We all knew that a Cincinnati audience is something special: there is great love for all the arts, and particularly music, in this city. Janelle and I were really ready for this performance. Johnnie recalled his days at the Conservatory in his introduction to this performance and then sang some of his most familiar songs. Janelle and I then finished the program with eight of the Niles-Merton songs and five other songs. Johnnie introduced each of them. He would sit by the piano, concentrating fiercely on the music, and sometimes he would turn pages for Janelle.

Johnnie had prepared some special material for his Cincinnati Conservatory audience, remembering his years there when he was in his late twenties, and of course the audience loved it.

JJN: When I came to this place fifty years ago, I had several songs in my portfolio. Everyone was amused. They thought I was just a funny little country boy from Kentucky who walked heavily on a cane and a crutch. I had been trying to fight a war to end all wars. My dear friends, it did not end anything — it pretty nearly ended me. I presently gave up the crutch — threw it in a fireplace — and walked on a cane. And I used the cane until the yogins in New York taught me a great many things, and they taught me how to walk straight, and I gave up the cane ultimately.

But as I came back to the Conservatory of Music with these songs, Dan Beddoe, my vocal teacher thought it was a great pity that I was so foolish to worry that these songs that did not end on "Do"— songs, my friends, had to end on "Do!" That's all there was to it.

[JJN sings] "Black is the color of my true love's hair." They said, "Well, where is it?" I said, "Well, that's the way it sounds to me. That's the way it is! And I'm telling it to you the way it is!" But they said, "No, no, no."

"Go Way From My Window" was — well, this idea of the man asking the girl to stay away from his bedside — you have no idea how prissy this place was!

At this the audience laughed and cheered.

JJN: There was no idea of a sleep-in, a love-in, a sex-in, no, no, no!

Johnnie loved being just a bit outrageous in this way, to let the young students at the Conservatory know that he knew a little about life and love and the pursuit of happiness.

JJN: But I sang the opera and worked myself into a state those first two years, and we had pretty good seasons for the opera. I sang the compremario parts and I'm sure if I'd wanted to be, I could have been a compremario till the end of my days, but I didn't want to be.

I felt that I wanted to carry out my father's instructions when he said, "The music came from the people, it ought to

go back to the people." It was very simple, wasn't it? A
simple statement, yes, but it wasn't easy to do because the
music I was singing was not commercially profitable. Not
until the end of the Depression— or the middle of the
Depression, when it was very, very, far down.

One of his messages to the students that evening was that
they must learn to follow their own inclinations, musically,
but never to expect financial success.

JJN: Presently I found myself on the Continent, singing in
Germany. My father never dreamed of that. He said, "If
you work at this stuff, little boy, you might carry it as far as
Cincinnati, or maybe Indianapolis."

Don't start out, my dear young people, to make a lot of
money out of music. You're not going to do it, unless you get
into some one of these things on Bourbon Street in New
Orleans — maybe you can make it there, I don't know, but
you can't make it in the legitimate way. I warn you— take
my warning.

Johnnie had tremendous energy and vitality as a performer: he knew exactly how to woo an audience and then
keep them fascinated. He was completely unaffected
about playing the Grand Old Man: he was seventy-seven
years old, and he was proud of it. He had no compunc-
tions about giving people advice and wisdom from the
vantage point of his age— he had utter confidence that
what he had to say was important, and he assumed that
everyone would be interested. He always told people bits
of his life story.

JJN: Seventy-seven years ago at sundown I was born in the
southeast corner of Jefferson County, in a sequestered quiet
little spot. I do not know how the stars were crossed, but a
reviewer not very long ago said I was the ugly duckling who
sprouted a swan's wings. Very comforting, wasn't it?

Then he would pick up a motif later in his narrative, in
true storyteller's style, and the audience would realize that
he was making a point.

JJN: *So the years came, and the years went, as years do. You know it's that way and very disconcerting sometimes when you realize that all of a sudden you're seventy-seven years of age and you wonder where all those years have gone. The duckling had sprouted swan's wings and I was using those wings from one end of the world to the other. It was NEVER profitable.*

At the Cincinnati 77th birthday concert, Johnnie told the audience about his great-grandfather: I believe he was explaining his musical heritage.

JJN: *My great-grandfather was a piano manufacturer and a player of Bach and Buxtehude. He moved up and down the Ohio Valley, from Pittsburgh to Cairo. He tuned organs and pianos after the War Between the States had destroyed his business. He tuned, and he played Bach and Buxtehude. He played in this town [Cincinnati] quite often in the Germanic churches. Because he was a German and never to the end of his days did he speak a very clear English. But he made a magnificent piano.*

His daughter married Jacob Augustus Reich, a veteran of the War Between the States with enough wounds on him— my goodness, if they would have given him stripes, his coat wouldn't have held them. But he was enormously lucky— he too was a German. Jake and Frederick Adams' daughter made a team— a rather pathetic start— she was fifteen when she married this man. He was in the hauling business. He was a man named Duckwall. I asked him one time, I said, "Grandfather, whatever became of Duckwall? He said, "Johnnie, you know they found Duckwall floating in the Ohio River face down one day." He and my father were like that.

Those were the days of delightful piracy. Nobody took much stock of what was happening in Louisville, Kentucky. The war was just over and the freebooters were loose. But my grandfather caused the Chickering Company in Cincinnati to send a piano down to the backwoods of Kentucky. It had

*to be dragged out there by ox cart. And there my mother,
who played Bach, Beethoven and Brahms taught me my
early music. She invented a way of teaching. I know this
now has meaning, by important teachers in the North —
when your children are so small their hands will just come
up to the level of the keys, they stand up and play piano, and
that's the way I played.*

*Father was a dancer and a singer and a wise guy, a political
fellow and a speaker who made wonderful political speeches,
God rest him. I used to stand on a soap box and sing three or
four verses of Barbary Ellen because I was such a curiosity at
age five, to attract people to his speeches. I had no loud-
speaker, no amplification. I wished through a few verses, and
everyone said, "Tommy, that's a sweet little boy you've got
there, and now tell us about the next election."*

The original plan for the program called for Johnnie to
make his introductory remarks, then talk about the dulcimers, then sing four of his famous songs. But Johnnie was
on a "roll," I guess you might say, that evening, and he
sang not only the four songs scheduled but also the three
ballads he was supposed to sing at the end of the program.
This turned the second half of the concert over to Janelle's
and my performance of the Niles-Merton songs and five of
Johnnie's love songs.

I had appeared with Johnnie in several concerts before, so I
had learned something of what to expect. We'd performed
some of the Niles-Merton songs quite a few times by 1969.
Johnnie was careful to change the tone and the pace of his
introductory remarks, to prepare the audience for a transi-
tion to a different kind of music. He would, as I said, sit at
the piano beside Janelle and focus on the music with
terrific intensity.

But we were getting familiar with his stage persona and
his narratives— and several of the variations on these.
When we shared the stage with Johnnie, we were "the
girls"— either sitting attentively or performing. It was
only natural that the entire focus should be on Johnnie.

When he said something outrageous, we had one of those "Oh Johnnie" looks on our faces.

At a Christmas concert at Transylvania University, Johnnie told an audience how his mother had taken him as a child to sing Christmas songs in a place called Jake Frank's Beer Parlor. Ten years later, he said, a Madam (probably the notorious Belle Brezing), asked him to sing a quartet on Christmas morning. He could really wake an audience up with these tales. Oh, Johnnie! They would gasp with surprise and delight.

It was at Bellarmine College in 1968 that we saw him go after a photographer for the first time. He sometimes scolded and shamed people who took photographs during a performance.

> *JJN: By nature I am not a tiresome person. (My sons say that I am very tiresome, but they're mistaken). But this little boy here— and that young man out there with the tripod could enrage me to the point of throwing the microphone at them! Sir, tie up your little machinery there. Don't walk in front of me when I'm trying to sing. Don't you know the public watches you— they lose interest in me. Now your photograph is never going to mean a dime's worth of any thing! [the audience laughs and applauds].*
>
> *See! I've got friends here in the front row. Bravo, boys! Bravo! Bravo! Bravo! At Gatlinburg Tennessee once I had a row of you. Oh it was marvelous! And they protected me from all harms and outrages. They conducted a standing ovation on things and they were prepared to throw anybody out of the house. Because I'm on these fellows' side, you know, when it comes to that one very tiresome cameraman.*
>
> *I thought we were going to have some fun there for a few moments!*

We saw Johnnie do this over and over, and it always worked. The photographers backed down in disgrace, and the audience cheered for Johnnie. It was exciting when he

Rehearsal at Boot Hill Farm
Photographer: Helm Roberts
Photo taken: 1969 ©

would interrupt the program like this to lecture— at length— anyone whose flash bulb had offended him.

But Big Corbett Hall at the Cincinnati Conservatory was an important place to perform. I remember how carefully I chose my gown for this performance. I thought of it as "Grecian" in inspiration: the material flowed gracefully in soft folds, and it was sleeveless, Jackie-Kennedy style. It was a great dress, and I felt wonderful in it. Janelle and I were both "up" for this performance, and I honestly think it was the first time that Johnnie had considered using us regularly in future performances. He could see that we could take the pressure of this kind of concertizing.

We began our portion of the program with the Niles-Merton Songs, nine of them, and from the very first the audience loved them and had no problem with the "existential" qualities of the words or the contemporary tonality of the music. They were a well-educated audience, and it was a thrill to sense how much they enjoyed these songs. We concluded with more familiar love songs, beginning with "The Lotus Bloom," which had a Cincinnati connection.

> JJN: *In nineteen hundred and nineteen I encountered a Chinese waiter in the Canton Restaurant downtown in this city, and he and I together translated several Chinese poems. He was a student at the University, studying English and studying law. The result of it all was "The Lotus Bloom." I turned the music over to a young lady at the Conservatory, and she— like the girl with "Go Way From My Window"— was amused. Never went to the trouble to sing it. Since then a great many people have sung it.*

Johnnie took advantage of his great age in telling stories I thought of as "Vindication" or he-who-laughs-last-laughs-best narratives. This he believed would be of special interest to young musicians and composers. At the Cincinnati concert, he told the story of "Go Way From My Window."

JJN: In 1908, when I was exactly sixteen years of age, I wrote a song for a girl who had blond hair— lovely of figure, beautiful of face. She had everything in her favor except good sense: she couldn't recognize a composer when she encountered one! I held that against her loudly. I wrote the song and gave it to her before I even sang it to her.

Well, it got back to me by the grapevine that I was no composer, I was no gentleman, of course I was no musician. Well I was a nothing person. I took this song very sadly and put it away. And the girl went on and married the other man, and that was the greatest benefit that ever happened to me. If I had married that poor little heifer, I would not be here tonight singing to you charming people. It takes a powerful woman to propel a man through a career on the concert stage.

However, I forgot all about her until she went on to greater glory and ultimately died in an automobile accident, and I didn't even go to the funeral. Had I been a student and a devotee of Zen in those days I would have felt differently about it. But I hadn't found out about Zen, so I took the song and put it away and it gathered dust for a long while.

Just when you began to think this is a story about a broken hearted lover, it would turn into a history of the song itself.

JJN: In 1908 it was written. In 1940, thirty-two years later, I took it out and carried it with me to my concerts I was singing on the continent. Those days were great days in Berlin. The roof had not blown off yet, and the Gefurstendamm was magnificent. And — well, it was a great period. I sang "Go Way From My Window" to a delightful group of people in the Bechstein Zalle and when I finished they got up and got out of their seats and came up to the footlights and shook my hand. That's the way they tell you in Germany that you've done a good job. My hand was practically destroyed! I had the greatest difficulty carrying on for the rest of the concert!

Then would come another plot twist, another roadblock to success.

JJN: I brought it back to the United States of America and, like my early experiences at the Conservatory with the songs not ending on "Do," the publisher said, "John, you're the most naive little boy in the world. How can we publish this and offer it to the public? They'll laugh us to scorn!"

But persistence is the name of the game, and so Johnnie never gave up.

JJN: Well, I took it down to the Metropolitan, and my friends down there — Eleanor Steber and Gladys Swarthout, Patrice Munsel and the other girls were very charming and cooperative. They took copies of the song out and sang it in their concert tour and that was it! The publishers came along. You should have seen them with their hat in their hand! Ha-ha-ha-HA!

It was published and now it's sung from here to the end of the world, just like "I Wonder as I Wander Out Under the Sky," in Tasmania and New Zealand, Australia, the islands of the South Sea. Just what they do with it out there in grass skirts I'm not sure. Japan, Nationalist China, South Vietnam. I know this because I get a small check from them every now and then, for the use of it. That's the surest way of proving that they used it.

So: "Go way from my window,/ Go way from my door,/ Go way from my bedside and bother me no more." She NEVER bothered my bedside!

He would often round off a story this way, returning to the beginning, reminding us of the girl that broke his heart in the first place, and then he would perform the song. But his stories had more layers to them than mere romance, and quite a few of them held the moral that you must believe in yourself and be patient (and tenacious) if you wish for success. Vindication! His pleasure in the final triumph was infectious, and audiences were eager to prove that they were not so narrow-minded as those who had criticized Johnnie along the way.

But he changed the tone for the performing of the Niles-Merton songs, and his outrageousness would take the form of his announcing yet again that he was not a Roman Catholic — if anything, he was a Zen Buddhist. Or he would declare, as he did at a concert in Memorial Hall at the University of Kentucky, that he was personally "violently in favor of peace." In 1968, during the height of the Vietnam War, this was still a fairly startling thing to announce. In fact, Johnnie advised the Cincinnati audience to study Suzuki's book on Zen.

JJN: You'll come to some remarkable conclusions, I think. Of course I know that I'm only a Boone Creek boy, and am very impressionable. But as they say in Hollywood, California, I had already seen the pictures. I picked up my first volume of Zen and I read through it, and then I read through it again, and now I have certain pages in it I've read twenty-five times, and I still don't understand the doctrine of "No Mind." Thomas understood it — he wrote about it. You'll hear it in the text of the songs Miss Roberts and Miss Pope are about to perform. I think you will agree perhaps that it is fresh and new and delightful, and you will also know that Thomas Merton tells it to you the way it is.

This is my soprano Miss Roberts. And yonder at the piano is my accompanist Janelle Pope. They have worked diligently with me a long, long time. The music was not easy.

As I mentioned before, this audience was full of music lovers. Johnnie introduced each of the Niles-Merton songs briefly. The songs were very well received, and Janelle and I were well received. The contemporary sound of the songs was pleasing to these people, as was the unusual nature of the poetry. I was thrilled and excited: Janelle was in great form. It was this concert in Big Corbett that made me realize what a great experience concertizing really is — you can get a tremendous "high" from it.

Then as a change of pace, after "The Lotus Bloom," I sang "I Have a Flame Within Me," "My Lover Is a Farmer Lad," "Unused I Am to Lovers," and finished with "The Wild Rider." All of these are more familiar, more popular compositions, and they were enthusiastically received.

We were staying in the Vernon Manor, an older hotel near the School of Music where visiting artists usually stayed. The morning after the concert, Johnnie, Rena, Janelle and I met downstairs for breakfast. I remember that someone from the hotel came in and handed Johnnie the reviews. This morning was marvelous because of the glowing review by Henry Humphreys in his "Music Beat" column. "Monday night's highlight— a garland of songs— with music by Niles to the verses of Trappist Tom Merton— their styles fused together by intense inner emotion. . . let wind-finger bestirred cantilenas— replace our dark miseries with love-filled novenas." Who could ask for anything better? It was like receiving another bouquet of compliments!

I think Johnnie was satisfied that he deserved this praise. But he was already thinking ahead to the music he was going to write for the next year at his seventy-eighth birthday concert.

VI

On Tour

The secret of Johnnie's tremendous stamina and energy
as a performer was his generosity. The annual birthday
concerts were his opportunity to make a gift of his music
to the people. His father had said that the music comes
from the people, so you must give it back to the people.
He poured his heart and soul into his concerts as much as
into his compositions. And he was rewarded mightily by
the enthusiasm and affection of the audience: it invigo-
rated and inspired him. The revitalizing cycle of a
musician's giving and receiving is one of the many important things I learned from these years.

When Janelle Pope's parents invited us to perform at their
home, Johnnie was delighted to oblige. Johnnie had often
made the point that the accompaniments to the Niles
Merton songs were inspired by the fine talent of Janelle.
He was very proud of those accompaniments. It was a
pleasure for him to be able to give something back to
Janelle in exchange for what she had brought forth in him.
Janelle's father was Judge Astor Hogg of Frankfort, and the
guest list consisted of a great number of their friends,
many of whom were in politics. It was a beautiful sunny

February day, and I remember how pretty Janelle's parents' home was: it was a one-story house, beautifully furnished, with a fine grand piano.

Johnnie put on a full-length show, complete with his dulcimers. My husband Helm came along and took a whole series of photographs that day. Johnnie was as generous with his music at this small-scale performance as he would have been in an auditorium. The Hoggs were proud and delighted that their daughter was associated with John Jacob Niles (and with me): the Judge and Mrs. Hogg in their thank-you note said that there had been "praise from every hand."

Johnnie's seventy-eighth birthday concert, held in Carrick Theatre at Transylvania University in 1970, was a benefit for the Lexington Philharmonic. This year I premiered four new songs: "Tuesday Afternoon," "Weary Nightbird," and from the courtship cycle, "Tender September" and "To Wake at Dawn."

Sometimes I felt as though Janelle and I were almost interchangeable in his mind. We were, after all, "the girls." For example, when the Nileses went abroad one summer, they would write to one of us and ask that we share the letter with the other. Here's an example of a letter written to Janelle.

> JJN: [Written from the Bag of Nails, a pub]. Share this with Jackie please. We have just been to the Changing of the Guard at Buckingham Palace. Saw royal equipage carrying representatives of some emerging African nation. Across the street is the Buckingham Palace Guard. [Rena notes: "The lady who tends bar has a little white cairn who sleeps at the corner of the bar."] We miss you all— wish I could carry you and a grand piano with me.

Here's another note, this one to me in January 1971 from Baker University in Baldwin City, Kansas, where Johnnie did a workshop and gave a concert. (Johnnie wrote "Symbol," a wedding song, there during his stay.)

JJN: Accompanists and sopranos, no one can touch you and Janelle or Nancie Field with a 10 foot pole.

My sister, Ruth Trumbo, was living in Charleston, West Virginia at this time. Johnnie had written a cantata, "Golgotha," which he was eager to have performed. Ruth for her part was eager to be helpful in bringing this work to the public, and so she made the necessary arrangements. The Charleston Civic Chorus was pleased to premiere this work. Janelle was unable to be a part of this program, so my sister arranged for Catherine Manning Walker— a wonderful pianist— to be the accompanist. "Golgotha" fulfilled Johnnie's desire to produce a big musical work inspired by some of the ideas he'd been working with in the Niles-Merton songs. "Where will we find peace?" was the question it addressed.

JJN: We crucified a Man of Peace who bucked the establishment. Where then will we find peace?

I never thought of this at the time, really, though it was in the back of my mind and emotional understanding, I suppose. Johnnie was still grieving the death— in his mind, the murder— of Thomas Merton. The cantata is in the Christian tradition, appropriate for an Easter service, but it certainly could also be a eulogy for his friend who had also bucked the establishment. It arrives at an answer to the question it poses.

JJN: We can find peace in the heart of the man of good will, the man who cannot hate anybody or anything.

Absence of hatred was something that Johnnie found in Zen Buddhism, and he associated it with the meditations that prepared him for creative work as much as he associated it with his friend Tom.

The Charleston concert was not limited to "Golgotha," however— it was really "An Evening With John Jacob Niles." I sang a sequence of songs, and Johnnie was inspired to get out his dulcimers and sing some of his ballads. It was quite a long program, and the Charleston review was critical. The headline read "LENGTHY CITY PERFORMANCE," so we knew we were in for it. Mr. Eaddy, the reviewer, declared that Niles "topped Brubeck" for going on and on. "Each of the three segments could well have stood alone as a concert." He reported that the concert began at eight, intermission was at ten, and then the cantata "Golgotha" ran for another forty minutes. "The audience got so carried away with Jackie Roberts that a standing ovation demanded an encore." Another standing ovation followed Johnnie's (and my) "Amazing Grace."

Needless to say, we were having a fine time that evening with all the standing ovations, but this review still makes me smile. Johnnie narrated the cantata and personalized his "interlinear comments" with his own observations and asides on various subjects, including racism and the "generation gap." By now I was completely at home with these Niles programs: anything Johnnie wanted to do was fine, and very little could happen on stage that would surprise me or take me off center. It was a lot of fun.

I remember a performance for the Sisters of Charity of Nazareth in Nelson County, Kentucky: this was on August 7, 1971. Johnnie was really thrilled by the audience of nuns. We were in the Nelson County High School auditorium, and I remember looking out over the audience and seeing so many black and white habits— it was like a sea full of penguins. I was no longer working with Janelle Pope at this time. Janelle had moved away from the area and thus was unable to continue as my accompanist, and I had begun working with Nancie Field, a pianist who had been born in Australia and had come to the United States as a war bride during World War Two. Nancie lived with her husband Tom and her two daughters, Julia and Gwen, in Lexington. She was intrigued by the music of John Jacob Niles and by our project, so that she was willing to work hard to prepare for this tour. She was eager to take suggestions and very anxious to learn as much as she could about it. I remember that she made a point of studying all of the Niles music and not just what we were performing at the time. Everyone was grateful for her perseverance and cooperation, which made this tour possible. She was my accompanist for many years after that, becoming as Rena put it, a member of the trio.

There was an upright piano on the high school stage that had to be placed in such a way that I was to sing from behind it: it was like leaning on a garden fence and singing to your neighbor. This was a little odd. But odder still, I had been taken off guard before the performance when a woman I'd never met came up and introduced herself. I had only heard about this woman, a soprano who had performed Johnnie's music a few times in years past, though she had never appeared on stage with him. Anyway, in the most unpleasant manner imaginable this woman said to me, "You know, I rightfully deserve to be in your place up there."

I was flustered by this. She sat prominently in the audience, where I couldn't miss seeing her, and I experienced some extra stress. I had always received so much affection from audiences, and I had always enjoyed sharing in these waves of approval, so it was a bit of a shock to be the target of a rude and envious remark.

We sang nine of the Niles-Merton songs, and the nuns could not have been kinder or sweeter. They hovered over us backstage and lavished gratitude on us— they even followed us out to the car. Johnnie was delighted and took Sister Marian Carpenter's hand and kissed it with a flourish. She blushed and laughed when he boasted, "I have just kissed a NUN!"

On the way home we stopped at Old Stone Inn, a restaurant near Bardstown, for dinner. I was still feeling a little queasy from the stress of performing before someone who had been so unkind and envious. I remember having no real appetite, but I was reading the menu when another guest came over to our table. This was a man who had been to our concert and had enjoyed it so much, he said, that if I would sing just one more song he would buy everyone's dinner! So I rose to the occasion and sang for my supper. The man was as good as his word— he bought five dinners! My appetite returned.

Rena published an article in 1986 in *High Roads Folio*, a Kentucky magazine, entitled "On the Road With John Jacob Niles." In it she told of the formation of our little group. "How would it be, he asked me (for I was then his concert manager), if we added 'the girls,' as they came to be known, to the concert program? We debated the pros and cons and decided it would be a good thing to do: it would reduce Johnnie's singing time onstage by about 30 or 40 minutes, and best of all, it would give him the chance to present a whole new facet of his musical work."

She continued, "Thus the trio came into being, though it was never called by that name. It remained to the end John Jacob Niles, with Jacqueline Roberts and Nancie Field. And it would be hard to imagine a more amiable, more congenial group of people. Because of the vast difference in age and experience, there was no question that John Jacob Niles got star billing. Everyone seemed happy with the arrangement."

Rena had a big job, planning and scheduling performances, arranging for tickets and accomodations, and much more. She wrote, "I was the tour manager, secretary, part-time chauffeur and part-time cateress. The props were my concern. And that meant not just four large dulcimers, each in its heavy black case, a music bag and the usual assortment of clothing. In addition, when we were touring by car, we carried a picnic hamper, a large cooler and innumerable baskets of provisions. Not only did we supply ourselves with orange juice and coffee for early morning in our rooms, we also carried the makings of a daily picnic lunch."

Our first stop on that tour was a small college in Cleveland, Georgia, Truett McConnell College. Rena had found us accommodations at the Gateway Inn. The town was as small as the college, so we were pleasantly surprised to find ourselves with an audience of between two and three hundred people, a mix of students and townspeople, many of whom had brought their children. Johnnie was always completely at ease with this kind of an audience. Typically, a baby would start to cry and an embarrassed mother would get up to take the baby out of earshot, but Johnnie would stop the show.

JJN: *Don't take that baby out of this auditorium. I love children!*

I remember that Johnnie was fretting a little about the Niles-Merton songs, worrying that they might be too sophisticated or too unusual for a general audience. But he need not have worried: this crowd was starved for music and they were fascinated with these songs.

We went on to Atlanta, where we were to perform at Agnes Scott College. Nancie and I stayed at the college's Alumnae House, because Nancie had a friend there. I visited my husband's brothers, Hank and Jim Roberts. Hank had been responsible for installing the sound system in the big new Atlanta stadium. He was so kind as to make a tape of our concert for me, something Helm usually did at home.

We performed at three o'clock in the afternoon in Presser Hall. John Portman, the architect who designed Peachtree Center, had also designed Presser Hall. My recollections were not architectural, exactly: it was really chilly backstage, where I waited, so I had to pace around to keep myself warm. But it was winter and I was wearing a formal gown, so I suppose it couldn't be helped.

The Agnes Scott girls were very charming and well-mannered. We'd lunched with some of them in the school cafeteria. We knew that this was one of the finest liberal arts colleges in the country, so Johnnie had prepared some special "interlinear" commentary which would further their musical understanding. He really opened up to this particular audience about Thomas Merton, Zen, and contemporary composers.

JJN: Is there anybody in this house who does not understand my diction? He is privileged— and I ask him, please, to go to the box office and ask for his money back. Whether you paid or not!

He talked about poetry, apologizing for not providing the text of the Niles-Merton songs in the program.

JJN: We had hoped to have the texts of these songs in your hands, but it didn't work out that way, quite. So I'm going to read you a few words of the texts from time to time. Miss Roberts has such fine diction, and the room being as good as it is, I think you'll understand it. And Nancie Field has grasped that elusive thing called sound— s-o-u-n-d. Her pianistic work is not a matter of plunk, plunk, plunk, plunk, plunk, one note right after the other. We don't consider that to be piano playing, if there isn't sound. Now I'll ask these two sweet girls to come on— are you there girls? Come on, that's right.

Johnnie's energy was high during this tour, and he was particularly generous with his Agnes Scott audience. After the Niles-Merton songs, there was an intermission before we returned to sing the songs of love and faith. While the audience was straggling in again, he addressed them.

JJN: In my performances, I never had an intermission, because my father— God rest him— was a very smart show business man and he said, "Never have an intermission. The audiences will go away and they may not come back." Tomorrow night at 8:15 I will be here, alone on this vast stage with three dulcimers, and I will try to sing my way through ninety minutes of music. That sounds like a long time, but I don't think it'll seem a long while to you, because I have been said to be both entertaining and amusing. (That may be just wishful thinking on my part).

Johnnie was impatient to get on with the show, and he addressed the stragglers directly.

JJN: I'm waiting until everyone gets in. How about it back there, girls, are you coming in or are you not? We have a quaint custom in the mountains of Kentucky. I'm sure they must have it in Tennessee and the other mountain states, Virginia and West Virginia. Men in that community are always shy of coming into a building and listening to anything. They stand at the door in a tremendous knot. People can't get in, and— you follow— they can't get out. My father, who was also a law enforcement officer, said he had worked out a plan to have a group of his deputies RUSH the door at some time or other. And of course there would be a confrontation and a great battle. He said, "I think they would go home and tell their people what had happened, and the door-standing would be over." But as far as I can remember, they're still standing in the door.

For the second half of the program Johnnie introduced, and I sang, songs of faith and then love songs. He was still focussed on the subject of music and poetry composition.

JJN: "The Flower of Jesse" was the first thing Miss Jackie sang from my catalogue. It was her introduction to my strange way of writing music. You will discover if you attach your attention to the accompaniment, you may discover that I write the accompaniment as if I were writing for a string quartet. I like to hear all four voices going and not just standing still— moving and getting somewhere, adding something vital to the support of the melodic line.

You do remember that this was the same concert where Johnnie said I was right off the mountainside next to the Ohio River. Anyway, when we came to the love song "December Morning" he told another story on me!

JJN: When first I exposed this love song entitled "December Morning," Miss Roberts, being a naive sweet thing, thought I had written a song she could sing at Christmas time in church. *"My soul was sated one December morning"*— she did NOT sing it in church on Sunday.

The Agnes Scott girls giggled over this, and I gave him an "Oh, Johnnie" look.

We went about writing these love songs with great care and philosophical consideration. We studied Martin Buber— Paul Tillich— all of the existentialist theologians. Strange that we would go to the theologians to study the technique of the love song or the love lyric, but that— I'd like to tell you young people— is where you find it.

Another chapter will tell about the love songs and the courtship cycle. For now, on the subject of Johnnie's generosity as a performer and his involvement with his audience, the conclusion of this performance at Agnes Scott was our singing of "Amazing Grace." When I'd finished "Wild Rider," Johnnie took center stage with his dulcimer, first to tell the story and then to lead the audience in singing. The story was a cautionary tale of the Forgotten Composer.

JJN: "Amazing Grace" was written by a little preacher in Baltimore. Now let's see, what was that year— 1801. No one paid any attention to it. Naturally. It got into several books of shape-note songs and was more or less forgotten until we got ahold of it— and the Baptists all over the country. We're not Baptists, but we know music when we see it. Or hear it. [Tunes the dulcimer].

We began to sing it about, here and there, and I suppose some Hollywood talent scouts who called heard us and said, "Ha-ha! Here's a number!" And pretty soon you heard it coming out of television boob tubes and radio sets all over the land, and it began to sell records right and left.

And the poor little fellow moldering in his grave in Baltimore gets nothing. But that's what it is. If you're going to be a composer, you've got to get ready for that, you know. There may not be any Baptists among you, but come on, sing it with me now.

The version that we sang involved a slight variation of the melody that today's audiences would consider unusual. It was fun when the audience sang with us for the last verses. Johnnie made a point of winding up his program with this Appalachian phrase:

JJN: It was awfully pretty to be with you all. God bless you and good evening.

Portrait of John Jacob Niles
Title: "I Wonder as I Wander Out Under the Sky"
Photographer: George Kossuth
Photo taken: 1942 ©

VII

On Tour
Dulcimers and Ballads

Between 1971 and 1975, we did some touring and
gave concerts in New York, Ohio, Kansas, and Indiana.
Johnnie was in incredible form for a man in his late
seventies and early eighties. Rena made her usual careful
plans, and NancieField-- who was not a part of the regular
team-- and I had some fine times. Shortly after we returned from Atlanta and the Agnes Scott recitals, we set
out for Colgate University. We drove to Louisville and
from there flew to New York. There was plenty of
excitement at the beginning of that trip when Nancie left
all of the music in the ladies room at the Louisville airport.
She quickly realized what she had done and was able to
run back and retrieve it, but not before she had totally
panicked. Since Nancie was a very responsible and organized person, the last person you would ever expect to
misplace something, we all thought it was funny. But
Nancie didn't recover for several hours.

At Colgate we stayed in a strange combination of dormi-
tory and inn. There were students coming and going all
night long, making noise. I heard dogs barking at all

hours. Nancie and I managed to get some sleep, but Johnnie the next morning was angry.

JJN: Outside my door some little girl was screaming, "Don't tear my pantyhose. They costed 79 cents!"

We performed in a gorgeous, charming, acoustically perfect hall. There were no problems whatsoever singing in this space. After the concert, we all met Dexter Marshall, a Colgate faculty member and composer who was exploring computerized composition. He proudly showed off his synthesizer to Johnnie, who was vehemently opposed to the use of this sort of technology in making music.

JJN: It sounds AWFUL!

Johnnie customarily talked about his dulcimers, and then performed some of the ballads he was known for.

JJN: This instrument I'm going to use is called a dulcimer [tunes]. One-one-five-one. [Demonstrates]. And then two fives, an octave more, and two ones. Now what do those lower notes remind you of? I hope they remind you of a tympani, because that's what I put them there for, because I was so fascinated by the tympani in the orchestra.

As years passed I found out about the dulcimer. As a matter of fact I found out about it from relatives of mine when I was extremely small, but I didn't have one of my own. Finally my father bought me one for a dollar and fifty cents— and got the man who sold it to vote for him. That's the way we handled our politics in Kentucky: my friends, I want to tell you, it's a fact!

As a boy, smaller than any of these little ones I see here, I heard Thomas' Orchestra from Chicago when they came to Louisville, Kentucky. My grandfather at that time was a tycoon in the city, a particular friend of German immigrants and musicians, and he entertained the entire orchestra. And they drank beer until they FLOATED AWAY in beer! They were such wonderful fellows. They let me go the next day to

*the performance and I sat among the tubas and the drums—
and I never was the same again.*

*I said to my father, who was an indulgent father. "Father," I
said, "I must have drums on the dulcimer." He wrung his
hands and turned me over to my mother. She said, "Well
you might as well let him do it— he'll do it anyhow." Just
like so [demonstrates] on this dulcimer, this cello in fact,
that's how I made this dulcimer. Well it was years— it was
years and years— I suppose fifteen, maybe twenty years
before I hit the idea. Creative ideas, you know, come to you
with such a bang. It's like a shock of lightning.*

*[Tunes]. Two strings, four strings on the other side of the
dulcimer. Originally the dulcimers were all this way.
[Tunes]. Now wouldn't you go a long way with that in this
big room? [Demonstrates with a small dulcimer. Laughter].
It'd be like whistling against a cyclone. I did add the other
string, and there I stood. And then when the Muse
prompted me, I went to work, made a wider keyboard, and
put on the other four strings. [Tunes].*

Audiences had expected dulcimers and ballads from John
Jacob Niles for decades, and he was always generous
about meeting their expectations. Rena had arranged the
necessary dulcimers in their special cases, to be ready on
the stage for Johnnie to tune. There were times when he
was still tuning these instruments right up to the beginning of the the performance, with ferocious concentration.

The least noise could distract and irritate him. Once in
1972 when he was preparing to perform as part of Lieuten-
ant Governor Julian Carroll's "Kentucky Arts Series," there
was piano roll music somewhere in the background during
the last half hour before the concert. Johnnie was so
aggravated by the noise that he insisted that it stop. But he
soon warmed up to the audience and they to him, and he
gave them a great show, demonstrating the "Nilesimers."

*JJN: This dulcimer is an instrument with eight strings on
it, and it's strung like this [tunes] one, one, five, one, and*

then two fives and two ones. The strings on this side are in every chord, and it gives you that droning kind of a quality [strums]. But if you can sing, you can make a pretty good use of it. You've got to be able to sing. Now this old dulcimer, I made this one, incidentally, out of half of a cello. My young son John Edward Niles, who plays the cello, first chair, cringes when I tell the story of how I sawed up a cello once. I would have starved TO DEATH playing cello! I was not much of a cellist. But once I got that instrument I was on my way.

He was proud of these instruments and loved to show them off, telling the audience how and for whom he had made each one. But he could also be disarmingly frank about his setbacks.

JJN: This strange looking thing I was carrying is called a dulcimer. The word is spelled d-u-l-c-i-m-e-r, a combination of two Latin terms dolce *and* amor. *For me, I've never found it having anything to do with "sweet love" at all. It's usually cut fingers, glue, shellac, varnish, disappointment.*

You should see how nicely these instruments burn, if you bend 'em over your knee and throw them in the fireplace. If they don't work, that's what I've done, because the average public is always so cruel with any kind of an inventor that they'll say, "Ha ha! I knew that fellow Johnny Niles wasn't any instrument maker." To prevent them from saying that, I just break them up and throw them in the fireplace.

Now [sings]"three-one-five-one" [demonstrates]— that's tuned really three-one-one, two fives and two ones. We have a way of saying in circles containing men who are foolish enough to try to make an instrument, we say the instrument "speaks." These lower tones— I think they speak. [Replaces the instrument]. No, that's rattling against the table, that's not in the act at all. That's extracurricular!

The portrait painted of Johnnie by his dear friend Victor Hammer in 1958 shows him in his white jacket, holding one of his dulcimers in his left hand and resting his right hand on the manuscript of one of his songs. The dulcimers were so much a part of his performing and teaching that I was completely stunned when— in the late seventies— Johnnie suddenly told me that I MUST learn to play the dulcimer. At the moment I flat out refused. As I've said, I never could imagine myself as a folk singer.

However, as events unfolded, in the years immediately after Johnnie's death, I was performing with dulcimers again and again. My cousin Charles Simpson made my three beautiful dulcimers, which I still use occasionally when performing "Bowie, Bowerie," "Black is the Color of My True Love's Hair," and "The Frog in the Spring." One of the dulcimers that Charles Simpson made is a replica of Johnnie's "little E" dulcimer. Charles photographed it, measured it, and produced a beautiful instrument.

I've shown Johnnie's dulcimers at a workshop at Northern Kentucky University, organized by Nancy Dysart Martin, where I also taught a vocal workshop coaching students in the singing of Niles songs. I sang with dulcimers at an Elderhostel picnic, performed at the Campbell House Inn in an all dulcimer program benefiting Volunteer Services, and sang with them again at the Christian Women's Club. For a while, I seemed to have gone "totally dulcimer." I can just imagine Johnnie's "Ha, ha, ha, ha, HA!" from the great beyond, when he remembers how I'd refused his— it was more than a suggestion, it was a— command!

I even played dulcimer and sang folk songs for a Crafts Fair in Louisville organized by the governor's wife at the time, Phyllis George Brown. And once I brought Johnnie's dulcimers to the Lexington School to show the kindergarten class of Harriet Collier. I demonstrated a bit, and when I told them how old these instruments were, I said that they even smelled old. Thirty little children promptly lined up to smell the dulcimers.

I sang a Niles program with dulcimers at the dedication of the new Kentucky State Archives building in 1982, and gave a Master Class and a concert of Niles music that same year at the University of Dayton in Ohio. My "big sister" from Oberlin days, Alice VanArsdale Hotopp, invited me to Dayton where I had a wonderful time working with her students. My accompanist there was a fine pianist, Brenda Brotherton. There was a handsome program for this concert showing me holding a dulcimer. I sang and performed with dulcimers in Lexington's Radisson Hotel, at a benefit for Senior Citizens.

After Johnnie's death, when Rena gave the John Jacob Niles Collection to the University of Kentucky in 1983, I gave a "Niles Collection Recital" at the University's Concert Hall. After that, I signed the dulcimers out of the University's Archives to take them to performances. These are just a few of the many Niles recitals I gave, complete with dulcimers. I understood intuitively, I suppose, that for audiences to see and hear Johnnie's beautiful custom dulcimers again was a way of commemorating the man who had been an important—and dearly beloved— part of the musical scene. He had stories about each of them.

JJN: That one was not intended to be a dulcimer to start out with. It was made for a girl in the north— when I say north I mean North-north above the Mason-Dixon line— whose people were rich and could afford instruments. And it didn't function in the beginning because it was too big. The girl was big, but not that big, and the result was that I took it back.

Her father, who was a rich man over in Massachusetts, had already paid me a handsome fee in advance. I hated the thought of giving that fee back— I'd already spent it. So I'd hoped against hope, and finally the girl said, "I want you to make me a smaller dulcimer so I can marry a man who's going off to Greece to teach in the College of Classical Studies in Corinth, and I want to carry along a dulcimer so I can play Greek folk music." She wanted to make more or

93

*less a guitar out of it. I finally turned her out a dulcimer
much smaller than this, and she went out there and had a
few babies and picked up a few songs. (She didn't really have
sense enough or skill enough to become a folklorist. It takes
more than— well, I can tell you it takes more. I know how
very much more it took in my case).*

*I took this back and hung it on the walls of my little
shop at the University of Kentucky. It hung there
many years, and I finally decided to saw it up, because
that's a magnificent piece of hair-grained walnut. And
this one once was, before they threw it off the top of a
truck, this was a fine piece of Carpathian spruce. And
this little one over here I use principally to motivate "I
Wonder as I Wander." It was thrown off a truck too in
the Washington Station once. I tell you, baggage men
have a way, don't they? But anyway, my associate said,
"Doc, don't cut it up. Let's tune it up." It turned out
pretty well.*

At his eightieth birthday concert, once again at the Patricia
Corbett Theatre of the Cincinnati Conservatory, Johnnie
made a special point of boasting that his pegs for tuning
the dulcimer had come from the Sears Roebuck catalogue.
I was unnerved at that concert, partly because the orchestra
pit was such a long drop from the edge of the stage. In
performance Johnnie rambled all over the whole stage,
often coming forward to the footlights to share a confidence,
and that night I was particularly nervous about the
possibility that Johnnie might fall. Another thing had
upset me that day: I had learned that a young man had
jumped off one of the high towers at the Conservatory. We
had seen police surrounding the area, and we learned that
the boy had died. In spite of my anxiety, I must tell you
that the birthday concert went off without a hitch.

Also that year, 1972, Johnnie gave a performance at Tates
Creek Elementary School, where my son John was in the
fourth grade. Johnnie loved talking to the children and
dancing around as sprightly as a cricket, encouraging them

94

to sing with him. Somebody made a "home movie" that afternoon, and I remember calling Mr. Allen, the principal, some time later and inquiring about the film: he located it in his basement.

JJN: In the teaching of kindergarten, one must not only teach, but one must entertain, amuse, discipline, be sweet too, comforting and all those things. I have experience in this process, and I love it very much. Little children seldom ever talk back to you— I mean kindergarten children.

President Robert Martin of Eastern Kentucky University was celebrating the tenth anniversary of his inauguration, and invited Johnnie to perform at a special concert. This was a festive performance involving a whole range of Niles music, and Johnnie was in fine form. Invariably, he made the same two points at every single concert.

JJN: Do not be surprised at my high voice. When it's functioning it's extravagantly high. If it's high tonight I can sing my songs without any trouble. It's always been this way, and praise God it remains so, because if it changes, I'd be in an awful fix.

Now for his second point.

JJN: I'd have to make my dulcimers all over, because the dulcimers are all geared to the voice. The voice is not geared to anything.

In the late fifties and sixties, folk music had become all the rage. Johnnie enjoyed one of the peaks of his career during this period. Dulcimers and Appalachian music were rediscovered, as scholars traced ballads still sung in the mountains all the way back to their medieval and Renaissance roots. In the late sixties and early seventies, when anti-war protesting was at its height, there was much interest in the history of the protest song.

Johnnie had been collecting songs of all sorts for decades.

JJN: I've been singing this kind of music now since 1908. Just add that up and you will come to a considerable conclusion.

He always explained where he'd picked up each song and what he'd done to it.

There were those detractors who tried to say that he was composing music and passing it off as "authentic" folkloric material. Some believed that he had tampered with existing songs in other ways, and would not admit it. But I thought he was always clear about his sources when he was presenting songs to the audience. He frequently began with "My Little Mohee," which he called his father's song, and then followed it up with "Fond Affection."

JJN: "My Little Mohee" was sung many times by my father— God rest him— who was a singer before me, a singer of sorts, perhaps. He was a dancer, a dance caller, a politician. He built small houses and somehow we managed to pay our bills. God rest him, he was singing it continually. All through my youth I heard it, and every time I get near a performance, I'm pretty sure to start with it.

"Fond Affection" came out of my mother's kitchen. God rest my mother, she died at ninety-six, playing piano with several musicians almost to the end of her days. My father had a group of men around him called the "Conspirators." They were politicians, trying to influence the elections in Kentucky. The Conspirators sang, drank, talked, consumed gallons of coffee and a certain amount of other liquids. They used to figure out exactly how many votes some poor fellow was going to get. Their principal mission in life was to defeat somebody. And they usually succeeded. Among them was a man who sang rather well, and I took down a great deal of his singing while he wasn't watching. And that was the only reward my mother had for the awful business of bringing these people coffee and food and whiskey out of a five gallon jug.

There's a very interesting way— maybe you all know about it— of extracting whiskey from a five gallon jug. You can't bend over and pour it out: you have a copper tube called a "thief" and you run it down in there and put your thumb over the top of it and bring it up and slowly let it trickle into

*a glass— the most beautiful mellow reddish yellow stuff in
the world. Oh they worked that to a standstill, but I came
out the winner.*

*My mother said I was having the worst upbringing a little
boy could ever have. Personally I loved it. And many years
later I went back through my notes and my memories and
brought up a piece called "Fond Affection."*

There's no doubt in my mind that Johnnie was a master
storyteller who loved to put a "frame" of context around
his songs, and often a frame around that. He could distract, amuse, inform, persuade, instruct, and delight any
audience with his interlinear commentary. When he paid
his respects to his parents, as he did in almost every concert, by referring to his mother's teaching him music and
his father's introducing him to politicians, he was identify-
ing himself to the audience.

BALLADS

When scholarly critics accused him of inauthenticity,
therefore, he was deeply insulted. One of his first prin-
ciples for any musician was knowing exactly who YOU
were, where you had come from, what knowledge you had
accumulated, and what you stood for. He always shared
that with an audience. He believed that the music came
from the people and you must return it to the people— this
was what his father had told him. Finally, music must be
performed with passion and conviction, "from the heart."

Once he offered to give a concert at a Kentucky college
which prided itself on its understanding of all things
Appalachian. He received a polite letter back from them,
refusing his offer, explaining that they were looking for a
program that was "authentic rather than interpretive." He
was, I think, quite properly angered by this. Johnnie
performed as a balladeer until the end of his days.

JJN: A ballad is a song that tells a story. Or to take it from the other point of view, a story told in song. Any of you young gentlemen who move on to graduate study, if you happen to take your study at Harvard, the very first thing in English Two, you will hear that definition. It is a definition created by Child and later by Kittredge and then passed on to whoever took over the department.

"Barbary Ellen" is the most tightly knit and best organized of all of our ballads. Any of you nice people who like to write about it, I recommend that you get a copy of this text, or go to the library and look up English and Scottish Popular Ballads, *Francis James Child. It's in ten volumes. You'll find "Barbary Ellen" in it, number eighty-four, and there you can model your ballad on the way some unknown composer and poet put this famous ballad together. It's about the most widely known and greatest loved of all of our ballads. "In Scarlett Town where I was born/ There was a fair maid dwellin'." You'll notice it starts out locating geographically where the ballad happened, the time of the year, the state of the weather, the people involved— and the dreadful consequences.*

Johnnie had a way of letting an audience know that, even though he did not display academic pretentiousness, he had the scholarly information and qualifications as good as anyone's in the folk music area— and he had been studying these ballads and other songs for a long time.

JJN: And now we come to the great classics, the so-called Child ballads. "Child" because of a man named Child— Francis James Child, who graduated from Harvard when it was called Harvard College, and went to teaching in the English Department— and died teaching in the English Department. He brought together what appeared to him and to other scholars the most monumental collection of popular song— the popular ballads of the Anglo Saxon people. It was English and Scottish: it went back in the notations to Denmark, Sweden, Norway, Finland, the Low Country.

Mr. Child never heard folk singing in North America.
He had a student who brought him in a short piece of
music she had taken down from a schoolyard in New York
City. There they were singing some scrap of this magnifi-
cent music. That was the only reference he made to singing
in the western world. In my time I found sixty-five of his
three hundred and five items, and I have been singing them
now, as I said before, since 1907.

At other times he presented further scholarly credentials,
by referring to courses he had taken abroad.

JJN: At the city college in London, England, I sat under the
famous savant, the famous authority on the minor poets and
the ballad. This course was laid out as "The Ballad and the
Minor Poets." For weeks we studied one single ballad, and I
wondered why it took so long. And then I discovered the
grim and awful facts about it. It was not a thing to be
discovered lightly.

One of the ballads that Johnnie loved to perform during
these years was "The Hangman, or the Maid Freed From
the Gallows." His interest in this ballad, he said, had been
piqued by hearing it sung by an old woman who volunteered the performance on one of his trips through the
mountains.

JJN: It came to us in part from an old woman in Texana,
North Carolina, a small village a little ways from Murphy,
one of the most crime ridden and dangerous places, I sup-
pose, in western North Carolina. Everyone said, "Don't
go—you'll get robbed, killed." We went. I carried the
dulcimer and my wife carried a basket of trinkets for these
people. She turned out to be the Lady Bountiful. I played
music and no one even raised their hand.

One of them gave me such valuable information concerning
"The Hangman." Though it was based partly on what she
did — she was a very old woman and dropsical at the time,
hardly able to stand — but she did stand long enough to do
quite a performance of "The Hangman."

Appalshop made a film, which was shown on educational TV, in which Johnnie performed part of "The Hangman." My description in mere words, I am sure, cannot do justice to the level of drama that he achieved with this song. He sobbed, he clutched his dulcimer— as if it were the hangman and he was begging for his life. He just loved singing this song. I remember coming to Boot Hill one afternoon, and hearing a great emotional outburst from Johnnie. Rena let me into the foyer and whispered, "He's just rehearsing 'The Hangman.'"

JJN: This is the way "The Hangman" seems to me. The girl is on the scaffold. Over her head a long way is a man with a noose in his hand and he's about to put it around her neck, and she's using every argument in the book to keep him from doing it, hoping to stay his hand. Her parents are coming! Her mother, father, brothers, sisters, aunts, uncles, cousins are coming up the hill to see the hanging. The crime must have been enormous. She begs those people for a small sum of money. The law of the land being what it was, she might bribe that man and he'd let her go free. Not one of them would help her!

Ultimately I found [at the University of London] *that the girl had been taken by the police because she had done away with some property belonging to her master. She was only a very simple girl living in the home of a great scholar. She was beautiful. The scholar's wife was not. The oldest triangle known to time. Before long the scholar, having a very valuable jewel, comes to the girl and says to her, "My dear, I'd like to have you take care of this. Put it away safely and keep it." And she did.*

She put it away safely but it disappeared. And the investigation proved that the jewel was gone. The girl was taken by the authorities and tried. And she was about to be hanged when a fisherman — now I know this sounds fabulous to the end — it's a piece of mythology of course – a fisherman fishing in the Irish Sea came ashore with his boat, and he observed a large fish regurgitate something on this bank. He went over to it and picked it up and carried it into the city to the judges. And it was the lost stone.

Now the truth comes out. The wife had thrown the stone into the Irish Sea to discredit the girl. The scholar was totally disgusted with the whole situation. He cast his wife into the outer darkness and happily took the girl in her place. One of the few great ballads with a happy background!

Johnnie took a lot of relish in another ballad about an old woman so vicious that when the devil came to take her, he returned her. "There was an old farmer went out for a plow / With a new sing naggle sing new."

JJN: Here's a case of the devil coming up to earth — I suppose he must come UP — maybe he comes down, who knows? He came up and he picked up an old woman and dragged her down to hell, but she was so mean he couldn't keep her. There is usually one old crone, one wonderful old gray lady— they're gray because their clothes get gray and then they get the same color as their clothes. It's because that homemade soap they use never quite whitens the clothes. These gray ladies are the type the devil took down to hell. If they're married they give their husbands a difficult time. They're very tiresome. They beat their children. They cook poor meals. They even kick dogs. The devil knew about this old woman so he came to get her. You will notice, of course, that the farmer thought the devil came for his oldest son who was obviously a skylarking young man.

TOURING

In the fall of 1973 Johnnie and Rena, Nancie and I traveled to Wichita, Kansas, where we performed in the Duerksen Fine Arts Center. This was an adventure I will never forget. About a month before the Kansas trip, I became ill with laryngitis. I couldn't get a note out. My doctor— Laurie Thomas— who was also Johnnie's doctor, would not let me make a sound until the rehearsal after we got to

Kansas. This made everybody a bit nervous, but Dr. Thomas truly knew what was best. I was at my best voice. Dr. Thomas and his wife Anne have been good friends through the years, and I have always been grateful for his saving my voice.

The four of us stayed in the home of Mary Koch, a lover and sponsor of the arts. This house was a large elegant Spanish style house filled with amazing paintings. I remember seeing Renoirs and old masters on the walls.

We were told that there would be a party for us in Mary's game room, but for some reason I thought it might have a billiards table or arrangements for card playing. I never expected it to be literally full of game! There were stuffed and mounted wild creatures everywhere. It was a dazzling display of the taxidermist's art: everywhere I looked there were the heads of all kinds of antelope, deer, and African animals. Even the table itself was trimmed with polar bear heads. Mary and her husband had enjoyed big game hunting around the world.

This was a time when it was the fashion for women to wear sweaters and long wool "hostess skirts" to parties, and Mary's friends were no exception. What I did notice, however, was that they were also wearing real blazing jewels. Mary Koch also made jewelry: she was wearing a huge chain around her neck, made of big links like hardware chain, and she told me she had made it herself of real gold. It was extraordinarily heavy.

I remember being astonished when Mary said that they never locked their doors at night, but then I thought to myself, "If she's shot big game in Africa, a burglar probably wouldn't frighten her." I complimented one of the dishes served at the party. I was told it came from the Wichita Junior League Cookbook, and when I woke up the next morning I found a copy of this cookbook outside my door.

In the guest room where I slept, even the bedcover was a

wild animal hide of some sort. I discovered that Mary stored fur coats in the closet of this room. Nancie and I had a lark trying them all on: there were fox, mink, chinchilla and sable and others I could not even recognize. Sleeping that night under the animal hide, I had such a vivid nightmare that I awoke on the floor of the bedroom. I was running, running for my life from packs of wild animals who were pursuing me. Of course, I did not mention this to our hostess the next morning, when we gathered for breakfast in one of Mary's breakfast rooms.

We were taken to dinner one night to a private club in Wichita, as the guests of Jamie Knorr's father, a close friend of Mary Koch. The restaurant was at the top of a tall building and the dinner was in a private reserved room with a wonderful view of the city lights sparkling against the broad horizon that I always associate with the West. Johnnie was in fine form that night, telling one of his "tall tales" after another.

From Wichita we traveled to Baldwin, Kansas, where we had scheduled a performance at Baker University. Baldwin was not a very big city. Nancy and I wanted to get our hair "done" for the concert, so we walked from our motel to a little white frame house where I had seen a sign that read "Beauty Shop." Gladys was the beautician— it was also her home. She told me, "If you can come in at 7 A.M. I can do it." I set out at 6:30 the next morning in order to get to Gladys' place on time. The atmosphere was straight out of *Steel Magnolias*: Gladys' friends came and went, gossiping and chatting of course, and when they left, they put the money themselves into her cash register. I had a fine time that morning and I was pleased with what Gladys had done with my hair. I would love to go back there and find that place, to see if it's still there. That tour was so much fun, I couldn't wait for the next concert, and indeed we toured occasionally for the next three years.

Meanwhile, unknown to me, my son John— who was then in the second grade— had come down with chickenpox. Helm's mother, Barbour Roberts, was staying with my family while I toured Kansas. They decided not to tell me about the chickenpox, because they didn't want to worry me.

Early the next year I gave a concert at the Indianapolis Museum of Art, which held a small but lovely recital hall: there was an audience of about two hundred people. I drove to Indianapolis from Lexington, because I was looking forward to seeing my dear college roommate from Oberlin days, Mary Ann Luardo Rufo. She brought a group of friends to the recital and had planned a reunion gathering to follow the concert. The museum curator, however, had arranged a special private reception that I was obliged to attend, so we never had our little reunion. I have regretted this ever since, because a few years after that, Mary Ann suffered cancer and passed away.

Helm and my son John (who was now fully recovered from the chicken pox) flew to Indianapolis for the concert, and we all drove home together. The plane trip was the big thrill for John.

In April, Johnnie's birthday concert— he was now eighty-one and proud of it— was held at the University of Kentucky. Johnnie performed, but so did others. Sarah Holroyd had organized the concert: the University of Kentucky chorus, which she directed, was featured in the program. Mr. and Mrs. Kiviniemi, tenor and pianist, performed as well. He was a voice teacher at the University of Kentucky.

I have a little remembrance from my own birthday party that year. It was the one and only time I have ever organized my own celebration, at the Lafayette Club, and I had a marvelous time. Johnnie presented me with a gift and a little note that said: "To our favorite singer. Singers are strange people, they have their own regulation, and belonging to God (as they do), will always live in a never never land of love."

That was an interesting season for me. I sang Niles songs at the Frankfort Arts Festival, right in Capitol Plaza. The site was beautiful, but I had to use amplification, and at that time I hated it. I think the reason had to do with the fact that these songs were "art songs" and a certain sensitivity to the words and dynamics was altered by the microphone. I sang at Rupp Arena that year as well. For non-Kentuckians who may be reading this, Rupp Arena is the heart and soul of Kentucky basketball, named after the famous Coach Adolph Rupp who brought the University of Kentucky Wildcats to national fame. I watched the Governor at the time, Wendell Ford, out of the corner of my eye as I sang "My Old Kentucky Home." I was having a fine old time until the band struck up the second verse. I didn't know the words! But neither did Governor Ford!

When Studio Players of Lexington undertook *The Grass Harp* that year, I played Dolly. I will always remember that show. Johnnie and Rena never missed one of my performances. They were right there opening night of the show, sitting in the front row. I felt real pride in my part in *The Grass Harp*: in fact, I thought it was the best theater I ever did. Sometimes I wish I could audition for it now, if a company decided to revive it, because I am now so much closer in age and experience to that character.

CHILDREN'S SONGS AND PROTEST SONGS

The city of Ashland, Kentucky had recently refurbished its beautiful old Paramount movie theater and turned it into a Fine Arts Center. They asked Johnnie to celebrate this transformation with a pair of concerts, one for children in the afternoon, and another for a more general audience that evening. Not long after that, Johnnie sang children's ballads at the opening concert honoring the new Jane Morton Norton Fine Arts Center in Danville, Kentucky on the Centre College campus. The new building was the star that day: it has fine acoustics and is a marvelous performance space. Johnnie sang "Carrion Crow" and "I Had a Cat," which he introduced in his own special way.

JJN: One of the things I sang with great success with my kindergarten children was this one-time English lampoon entitled "I Had a Cat." It has been said— I shall not stand in a court of law and raise my hand and say this as a fact— I'm merely reporting rumor. It has been said that this was once a lampoon directed against a man as great as Oliver Cromwell. I never thought much of Oliver Cromwell. A great many English people agree with me too. However, he was the Lord Protector or President or Governor or whatever he was for only a few years, and he died and his son failed to carry on after him. The English people disliked him: I mean, a great many English people disliked him enormously while he was in office. They wanted to get him out of office and restore their king. At least that's the way the history books tell it.

They couldn't carry signs and banners as young people do now. It would have been rather dreadful — they might have lost their lives. So they made up a song. And this is one of the first protest songs in history, as far as I can tell. I haven't gone into the study of the protest songs, but I believe this is one of the early ones.

Many young people in this period of time who have gone in inordinately for protest think that they're singing the first protest song – or the most important protest song on record. The protest song started a long while ago. I propose to make a study of them. I can go back as far as 1642 and tell you there was a tremendous reason for protest song when Oliver Cromwell managed to take over the reins in England, and did such a pitiful job of it. The people disliked him and he disliked the people. He proved that by destroying sculpture and painting and fine examples of architecture, and forcing the British to give up their celebrations and to stop stuffing themselves at Christmas time and other times. Of course he didn't last long because God was watching him all the while.

It started out with a verse about the hog. It compared this unfortunate man to a hog — and then later to a mule. Well, the Americans got ahold of it and they added a great many things to it— a great many animals to it— because you could just not continue to sing a song about a hog, you had to do something else with it. The little children felt that the hog was a little too brutal, or too bitter, or whatever else hogs are.

I personally like hogs. Being a farmer's boy, I understand the hog well. I think it's a great creature— supplies us with wonderful food products. But it's also inclined to be a little messy, a little dirty perhaps. Stinking even, in the warm weather, the pens are. I know quite a lot about 'em.

He would flatter the audience a little for their lack of snobbery and ability to have a little simple fun, and then he would persuade them to join in and sing with him.

JJN: Now, my dear sweet people, I can't sing this song in greatly populated and sophisticated places in the Northeast — places like New York City, bankrupt though it is. They find me ridiculous singing about a hog and making noises to imitate a hog, because that's what I'm going to do. But schoolchildren, little ones, particularly in the kindergarten, they love this song. They have sung it over and over. I sit on the floor, the dulcimer in my lap, and together we sing "I Had a Cat/ The cat pleased me."

The thing is accumulative. Now I'm going to ask you, if you don't mind, to help me sing it. This is what I do: "I had a cat." And you all sing, "I say Fiddle I Fee." Now let's rehearse it.

Invariably the audience would be timid and slow the song down. Johnnie anticipated this, and would stop the proceedings.

JJN: Now my dear people, let me give you one of the experiences I have had with ensemble singing. When a great group of people (such as you all are) sing in unison voices, you usually go more and more and MORE slowly until it goes to sleep, because you're expecting the person next to you to sing. "I said Fiddle I Fee." No holding back. Here we go.

The other protest song he loved to perform was "Frog Went Courtin' and He Did Ride."

JJN: Now the other protest song that is eminent throughout the world is one that was written to shock the great Queen Elizabeth the First out of marrying any one of twelve young men who were courting her at the moment. Then came a young gent from France named the Duc d'Anjou, who was blood brother of the king then reigning in France. And he had all the proper recommendations, and the Queen received him with a great party and all this kind of thing, and the Scottish people went over the side at once. They thought, "Oh my goodness, here we're going to have more of these foreign princes in this country trying to take over. And the Queen will die and he'll be King— oh no, no, no."

Well, again, they couldn't go down to London and carry placards around her palace. Their heads could be decorating Tower Green the following morning. So they wrote a song. The Frenchman was the Frog and the Mouse was the Queen. And now my people took those nice verses and made them over. They turned them into six couplets with some nonsense refrains. In the state of Texas where practically everything is bigger than it should be, they have three hundred and fifty versions of the frog song in their archives.

But two were enough growing up for the Niles family. We have used both of them in the suite my son played here the other night. The first one is a highly organized thing concerning the frog courting the mouse. Now many of you young men who were contaminated by the United States Army of America (as I was), you will know that in France the English and the Americans irritated the French as much as they could by calling them "frogs." It was a disgraceful thing to do because the French are a great nation indeed. The French prince turned out to be a frog of course. He didn't make any progress with the Queen at all. According

*to the records, he was sent back to France with his tail
between his legs and that was the end of it.*

*My mother's kitchen on the farm was a place where every
thing was debated, torn apart, put back together, made over.
We thought it was better when it was made— I don't know
whether it was or not — but we took those verses and
made six verses in our own way, and added some gibberish
repetition. In the middle of it all it seems that the frog had a
sore throat or a cold or some kind of difficulty that according
to tradition could be improved by a little alcoholic beverages.*

*And the verse is "He took him a swig of corn whiskey." I
sang it that way once in the United States, I mean out there
near Chicago somewhere, and a group of people that were
very strongly WCTU [Women's Christian Temperance
Union] took ahold of me and almost threw me in Lake
Michigan. So I gave up this reference to alcohol, and we
interpolated the words "Sassyfras Tea." Now Sassafras tea
and whiskey look exactly alike. They're not quite the same
in effect. "There was a frog lived in a spring, sing twiddle,
widdle widdle widdle wee. He was so hoarse he could
not sing."*

These were the songs and stories audiences had come
to expect from Johnnie, and he was always generous in
giving them what they wanted. His schedule was quite
full in these years, and though performing was stressful
and made considerable demands on his strength, he
seemed always to gain energy from his audiences.
Though he might mope at times or brood about death,
though he might complain bitterly in private about
the limitations that aging imposed on his life, there was
no better remedy for Johnnie than a live enthusiastic,
warm-hearted audience.

CONCERTS OF 1975

We gave a concert in Huntington, West Virginia in 1975, where there was a handsome center including a gallery for displaying art and a recital hall that held three to four hundred people. This was one of a very few times in my career when I had the opportunity to perform in an area that was close to my home town, so the occasion was very special for me.

As a high school student I'd taken the bus every week to Huntington, changing buses in Ashland, Kentucky, to study with Marguerite Neekamp-Stein. She was a fine teacher, who had been trained at the New England Conservatory. I'd begun studying voice with her at the age of thirteen. I also also took piano lessons in Huntington, studying with Mary Shepp Mann, a superb musician who wanted me to become a piano major. So many memories came back to me when we performed in Huntington: I was happy to be returning my music to the community where I'd learned so much as a girl.

The group traveled to SUCC, Cortland College, in New York state, where the Niles' son, John Ed was teaching music. Johnnie gave two days' worth of concerts there, with everything from his ballads and protest songs to songs from his composed collection including the Niles-Merton material and "The John Jacob Niles Suite." He had brought all of his dulcimers. I remember the way Johnnie chose to introduce us.

> JJN: *According to my records, my young ladies are supposed to sing now, I think— yes. Hello, girls. This is Mrs. Roberts — Miss Jackie — and there is Miss Nancie in that lovely peach colored dress. They are going to sing love songs I have written especially for them and according to tradition I stay on the stage and turn pages. The fact that I wrote the music and the text doesn't mean a thing at this moment. It's all up to Jackie. Now, if you'll pardon me a moment, I'll move this away from you so you will not have to sing over too much debris.*

He was busy reorganizing the stage to clear the way for us. All of a sudden he nearly slipped and fell, but he recovered his balance and laughed with the audience.

> *JJN: There's a crack in the stage floor and if I disappear suddenly — I warn you, I'm not trying to do a "Houdini"— I'm merely answering the call of gravity. Is that all right, Jackie?*

"That's fine," I said as nonchalantly as I could manage, though my heart was beating like a drum for fear that Johnnie would hurt himself. But he had regained his composure before I did, and went on to introduce four sacred songs— "What Songs Were Sung," "Softly Blew the East Wind," "Sweet Little Boy Jesus," and "Jesus, Jesus Rest Your Head."

He was proud to point out that "Softly Blew the East Wind" had just been completed recently. Over the years, his audiences had always loved being treated to his latest compositions. In fact, he had dedicated this song to me. At the top of my manuscript Johnnie wrote: *"This copy for that Sweet Girl Jackie Roberts— who has helped me so much by being willing to try to sing my compositions even when they were as difficult as possible— almost unsingable, dull, or even obtuse. The advantage I have in the case of Jackie's voice is that I (without boastin' or braggin') know exactly where her voice is."* Then he drew a treble clef and marked a high "G" with an arrow, adding, *"This is her greatest note."*

> *JJN: "Softly Blew the East Wind" hardly has the ink dry on it. I did it in the last two or three months. My eyesight being what it is, I had a terrible time getting the manuscript going, maybe because I organized it for four voices, SATB, and for three voices, SSA, and finally for Jackie as a solo.*

It was also in 1975 that I sang the role of Lucy in the Lexington Musical Theater production of "The Threepenny Opera." On opening night, Johnnie and Rena were there in the front row. This was great fun for me, because I have enjoyed and participated in all forms of musical theater since I was a student at Oberlin. I love the convergence of drama, music, and poetry, and always have. The dramatic element in so many of Johnnie's songs always appealed to me.

This busy season was crowned in one sense with the unique recital at the University of Kentucky's Newman Center, in which we performed all twenty-two of the Niles-Merton songs in one evening. Nancie Field's mother had died, and Nancie had to go to Australia, so Julie Nave stepped in as my accompanist. She was the wife of Bill Nave at the time, who was active in Lexington Musical Theater. We only had about four rehearsals together before the recital, and Julie, a fine pianist, did a remarkable job. This was the only time that all of the songs were presented in one performance: years later, at Holy Cross Monastery, all twenty-two songs were sung— but in three separate recitals.

It was a rainy night, and there was standing room only at the Newman Center. The words of the songs were projected on a screen behind me, which I thought was a very effective device. Father Elmer Moore of the Newman Center introduced Johnnie and set the tone for the evening, saying, "Tonight we're going to sit and listen to and meditate upon twenty-two poems by Thomas Merton put to music with great genius by John Jacob Niles. It's going to be a different kind of an experience. What we're trying to do tonight is to enjoy beautiful ideas put in exquisite language, sung to music which interprets this language as beautifully as the language is written. The prime mover, of course, in this program is John Jacob Niles, who in his graciousness has asked that this first presentation of the full song cycles one and two of the poetry of Thomas Merton be done in a Roman Catholic Church. I would like to introduce to you John Jacob Niles."

I have already discussed the "I am not a Roman Catholic. . . I am a Zen Buddhist" portion of Johnnie's introduction.

He explained that he kept writing songs until there were twenty-two of them.

JJN: Finally we had all these twenty-two songs. And we have twenty-two because in numeralogy I am a twenty-two. I know that sounds crazy, but Rabinadrath Tagore told me that and I believed it.

He went on to give an oddly moving commentary on artists and madness, concluding with a text of his own in which he seemed to describe himself as King Lear.

JJN: Most people think that poets and composers are queer insane — to say the least. My father, God rest him, was a man of great philosophical attitude. He said to me, "Johnnie, listen, boy: if you're crazy and you know it, that's all right." He said, "If you were crazy and didn't know it, it would be awful. That's what you want to look out for— those other fellows."

So I have a few lines here in defense of the crazy Johnnie Niles.

"And again, on any smoky September afternoon, if you see me wandering aimlessly about with wheat-straw or barley entwined in my white hair, do not be concerned to the point of general alarm.

And again, on any smoky September afternoon, if you see me stumbling in an aimless way wearing only a meager part of my clothing, life will go on without the ringing of bells.

And again, on any smoky September afternoon, if alas I am tripping myself as I walk, terrified and red-eyed with abject weeping, do not raise your voice to call the guard.

And at last, on any smoky September afternoon, if you see me groveling on the ground, lacerating my hands and my knees on small stones, perfoming a long-over-due poetic penance, be kind to an old man who bitterly

regrets that many times he is without the benefits that
are accrued from reason, logic and sound sense."

JJN: I admit all of this, and I'm rather proud of it.

Reading this now, I am once again moved as I remember
my friend and mentor who could fall to his knees clutch-
ing his big dulcimer, pleading for mercy and sobbing with
grief as he performed "The Maid Freed From the Gallows."
I knew that some of the usual miseries of aging were
bothering him, and I knew that he could dwell at length on
the subject of death when his spirits were low. I knew that
there had been some difficult times, and Johnnie surely
knew that even more difficult times lay ahead, but I can
remind myself that even in his most aggrieved King Lear-
like outbursts, Johnnie was always "rather proud" of his
creative madness, no matter what anyone thought about
him. It was a matter of principle with him.

VIII

Composed Songs

The bicentennial year, 1976, was a memorable one for all of us. Lexington had rebuilt and refurbished its wonderful old opera house. This was a theater that had seen many glittering productions and legendary artists over the years, but it had fallen into disrepair in the sixties and seventies as it declined into a movie theater— and from then into disrepute because of the kind of movies that were shown there. When its roof fell in one day, there were those who saw it as an act of God to warn sinners against pornography. Others were startled and unhappy that a fine old landmark had become so delapidated, and began a campaign to restore it to the luxurious condition of its finest days.

A Niles concert was scheduled as part of the Grand Reopening festivities, and we were all thrilled to be a part of this marvelous event. I knew I had to have a wonderful dress to wear, so I shopped until I found the perfect one— a Victorian gown of the sort Jenny Lind might have worn when she sang in the Opera House concert a hundred years earlier. It was a charming cream-colored dress with a high neck and long sleeves and many beautifully embroidered details, like lace and tucks and inserts.

The Opera House is one of the nicest places to sing, because the audience enfolds you and surrounds you. It is not a huge gymnasium style auditorium: balconies and boxes along the sides of the auditorium make a wonderful "encircling" of the stage. When all the seats are filled with a warm adoring audience, as they were that night in May, performing there is a pleasure. My son Bruce was awestruck and said to me later, "I can't believe that this is my mother singing on the stage of the Opera House!" (The boys did not attend many of my concerts).

The artist Henry Faulkner shouted, "Bravo! Bravo! Bravo!" at the end of the concert, and rushed to the stage with roses which he presented to me. I was a little surprised to see crumbs of black dirt scattering onto the stage floor, and then I noticed that he hadn't handed me a bouquet at all— he had, he told me, uprooted an entire rose bush.

The Lexington Herald Leader had given attention to this event: John Alexander had written an article about Johnnie before the concert, and Virginia Boyd Cox reviewed it afterward in "Niles Concert a Joy." Johnnie was riding a crest of warm approval. Later that year, Irene Reid, writing a profile of Johnnie for the Louisville Courier Journal quoted Johnnie as saying that he was "the leading folk singer of the western world. . . you might as well admit it, I started the whole thing."

> *JJN: I am forever set upon— I suppose as any composer is, I being only a very humble small composer—I am set upon by nice people who want to know how composition is done. If I knew that, I'd write a book about it. And I could sell many copies in a month, I think.*
>
> *There are no rules. Oh, there are certain rules to composition, of course. But to start out from scratch and create a song where you are required to write text and tune—there you have a responsibility. It's perhaps fortunate that I am not always in possession of a handy text. Because as the text*

develops, the melodic line develops, and vice versa. The melodic line develops the text for me sometimes.

Recently a very important church in Lexington, Kentucky wanted a special piece of music for their Christmas service. And their choir mistress (who is a Minister of Music, incidentally) said, "Johnnie, write me a piece of music that could include children and grownups— two choirs."

I said, "Oh, very well. I will try."

"This is a commission: we mean to pay you for this." Oh my! Composers are not used to being treated this way!

I said, "What text do you want me to use?"

"We haven't got any text." I had to write the text and write the tune and do the arrangement for these little voices, and I did it. And to my great surprise, the day I finished the manuscript and handed it to her, she handed me a check! I nearly fell in the street! That's not the way composers are treated, you know. They usually hold the bag!

On the fourth of July, 1976, the bicentennial celebration was at its peak. The Immanuel Baptist Church in Lexington presented a cantata that Johnnie had written expressly for them entitled "The King and the Common Man." The Immanuel Baptist choir was directed by Bill Williams. I thoroughly enjoyed the experience of working with them, and with the church's superb organist, Daniel Tilford. The cantata had some fine sections and certainly was appreciated.

We also gave a concert at Ashland Community College in late November of that year. When I recall those concerts, I think often of how much Johnnie tried to explain his process of composition: each song had its own story, it seemed. A story that he told at Cortland College is typical.

JJN: A great many years ago in Hardin County, Kentucky — that's the county containing Fort Knox, incidentally— long before Fort Knox was ever dreamed of, I was in that county with my mother and other members of my family.

We encountered a group of people who had some "tore-down"— a term meaning "torn down"— some "tore-down" relatives. They had the "porelies" all the time. That is to say they were continually feeling badly— "the porelies." (They were a mother and two daughters living together for too many years without any men around 'em).

Somehow or other, my mother, who was awfully smart musically, managed to get these people to sing a little song that was well known in the community at that time. I don't know whether the song that Mother took down and put in her pocketbook, and kept until I was about fifteen years of age, kept all that time in her pocketbook— I don't know whether it was exactly what this family sang. I'll never know because they were long dead.

I took the fragments of music— this was a perfect example of how a carol or a folk song is created. I told a man last night in an interview that you get certain elements of music from the singer himself out there on the hillside, and you put it together. Sometimes you have to take it apart three or four times and put it together again. Ultimately you manage to bring something off. And that's what happened here.

"Jesus, Jesus, Rest Your Head." I have an idea that many people in this audience have sung this song in the form of a four part chorus in churches. "Jesus, Jesus rest your head/ You has got a manger bed." Now notice how already these people were contemplating the social changes that we're going into – listen. "All the evil folks on earth/ Sleep in feathers at their birth." But not Jesus — he had no feathers. He slept in a manger. And these people were setting it forth boldly.

Johnnie was criticized by some purists for being evasive in these explanations of his: they may have wanted the kind of scholarly exactitude that ballad scholars in the universities at that time were practicing. The vagueness of the "Jesus, Jesus, Rest Your Head" story was the kind of thing that annoyed some people, involving fragments of music, people who may or may not have sung the song, and a scrap of music from his mother's pocketbook. I believe that Johnnie's point in telling these stories was never to delude or to deceive, but rather to try to explain some of the mysteries of creative activity as he experienced it.

One such "composition story" recalled his experiences in the first World War, like the background on "The Blue Madonna."

JJN: *My commanding officer in the United States Army Air Corps gave me the responsibility of engineering and protecting and being sure that a certain group of young soldiers on commission would come back to camp all in one piece. They ofttimes sent me into countries where I could speak the language and generally it would keep our men from causing a condition that would cause the State Department some trouble. (That happens all the time whenever you have Americans wandering around in a foreign country with more money than they know what to do with).*

We landed— this commanding officer sent me away with this group, and we landed on the border between France and Spain. And we went over to Spain. The transport had no right to go at all, but the Spanish guards were delighted with a few cigarettes. We decided to go to this little village near the border where they were going to have a bullfight the next day. It happened to be the Fiesta of the Blue Madonna.

On that day, according to legend, sometime long, long ago, there was a bullfight. And the Blessed Mother and the little baby Jesus went to the fight, and Joseph was one of the matadors. And after the fight was over, he comes back out of the ring with his ribbons and honors and they walk on home.

As I said the other day in explaining this strange piece of music, it takes a lot to believe that. It isn't easy to absorb it, I know that, but if you're a Spanish Catholic and you've been brought up in that area, you believe it all right. They believe it quite firmly and sincerely.

Our boys of course fought with the gendarmerie, and they fought with the local people, and we had difficulty getting them out of trouble. But we had a young handsome extravagantly smart young Catholic priest who spoke better English than we did, and he got us out. And everything turned out quite nicely.

While the bullfight was going on, in my mind I heard, "To the ring came Mary, to the ring came Joseph, with the infant Jesus, to the Festa of the Blue Madonna." I even heard some of the music that night. I wrote it down and here it is.

Another song of faith that Johnnie set to music was the carol "I Wonder As I Wander." People have complained to me about the poor grammar in "For poor ornery people like you and like I." Johnnie always claimed that the text was rather a mystery to him too— nonetheless, he had quite a tale to tell about its inspiration. He was in Murphy, North Carolina, in 1933, where he encountered a "situation" in the town square. A family of evangelists— the Morgan family— were being ordered to leave town by the police, and they insisted that they didn't have enough money to do it. They wanted to hold just one more meeting.

Annie Morgan (Johnnie said that she was a lovely, disheveled, unwashed blond) sang a few lines of "I Wonder As I Wander:" Johnnie tried to get her to sing more of it, and he paid her a quarter for every attempt. Two dollars later, he still had only fragments of melody recorded in his notes. He went home and wrote additional verses and developed the original music.

JJN: Night before last on this platform, my son and I performed the suite entitled "The John Jacob Niles Suite," and it involved, certainly, "I Wonder As I Wander." "I Wonder As I Wander" has been discussed too often by uninformed folk. It reminds me a little bit about a situation I heard about in Lexington, Kentucky at the University a little while ago. There was some very perplexing problem about

120

the campus that had been discussed and discussed— and finally CUSSED!

"I Wonder As I Wander," although it may not have been cussed, it certainly has been discussed. No one has ever been able to explain it to me, although I wrote the music and arranged it, the text— and I re-wrote the last two verses of the text— I still don't understand it. I just have intelligence enough to accept it the way it is. Because the people in the far world seem to understand it.

He would always emphasize that the people could understand it, even if the scholars could not.

JJN: This carol has gone to the ends of the world, been translated into thirty-two languages, and sung everywhere. I admit I don't understand it, although I wrote it. A little bit like Thomas Merton and Zen.

At other times, he would just express annoyance.

JJN: "I Wonder as I wander out under the sky" has been explained too many times, I might almost add, by uninformed people. It's even gotten into the press that way. I think it tells its own story pretty well.

Not long after his April birthday in 1977, when he was eighty-five years old, the National Music Educators Conference honored Johnnie. We all went down to Atlanta to perform. It was a typical national conference, with lots of things going on at the same time. We performed in a good-sized hotel conference room with carpets— one of the worst places in the world to sing. I remember that the piano was not outstanding either.

But that didn't matter so much, because the audience was full of fond affection for Johnnie. After the performance, I remember, so many of them were eager to meet him and express their appreciation for his music. It was a love fest, and we all had a marvelous time. The organization presented Johnnie with a beautiful dulcimer that had his name on it. This was not a full-size functional dulcimer, but a wood carving of a dulcimer, suitable to place on the mantel.

Later that year, in November, we revisited Kansas City and enjoyed another warm welcome. Johnnie regaled his audience with more of his stories. The song "Go Way From My Window" had quite a background to it. You will notice that it involved another blond girl.

JJN: When I was sixteen years old (and since I was born in 1892 you can count how long ago that was), I was buxom, yea, buxom, blithe and debonair. And I was greatly enamored by a young blond female with blue eyes.

At this same time, my father had employed me— by way of summer employment— to work alongside a great black man named Objerall Jacket. That means Overall Jacket, and that was how his name was in the paybook. A man worked for a dollar and a half a day in those days and went to work at an early hour. The sun had been up for only a little while, and we worked until sundown. Objerall was a magnificent fellow: he would work and sing at the same time. He had about four words of text and a very limited amount of material. He sang, "Go way— heh-heh— by my window. Go way— heh-heh— by my door."

Well, after I had listened to this for some months, I said to myself that this was more than human nature could stand. I'll have to do something about this. I'll have to go over and ask him to give it up entirely.

But the girl, you know, solved my problems. She fascinated me to the point where I simply had to make her a gift. At least I thought so. I wrote her a song, "Go Way From My Window." She didn't think much of it. The news got back to me that I wasn't much of a composer. I was no poet, though I had written this. And certainly no catch as a husband, thank heavens for that. Had I married that poor little heifer, I would never be on this platform singing to you lovely people tonight. I'm not using big words here. I'm telling you truly. I consider this a public career. You are the public. I am your servant, you see.

"Go Way From My Window" I put away in a little piano seat. In those days — I haven't seen them up in this country — but in those days in the South we had a bench about that long, the lid lifted up and came back. Inside there went everything you didn't want. That's where the manuscript for "Go Way From My Window" slept quietly from 1908 until about 1930, twenty-three years. Then I pulled it out and reorganized it a little bit — not enough to make any difference — and carried it with me on my continental tour.

Then he told once again about the song's discovery by Eleanor Steber and Patrice Munsel, as he had at his birthday concert in Cincinnati in 1968. He loved the fact that this song had become so popular everywhere, after his childhood sweetheart— and several publishers— had rejected it.

At these concerts I sang, and still sing to this day, "Unused I Am to Lovers." I never tire of the story that Johnnie told about this song, and Rena tells it now, or I tell it myself when I perform it to this day.

JJN: 1931 found me playing harpsichord in a Belgian circus in the Walloon country south of Brussels. There was a space between my concerts in London and the ones I was going to do in Paris. In show business talk I was "at leave." So I played the harpsichord, and I played as well as I could. The harpsichord requires a good deal of repairing— all harpsichords do, and the news got around that I was a rather good harpsichord repairman. I was possibly better at that than I was a performer.

Yes indeed. A harpsichord in a circus. I landed in Belgium and discovered not only a harpsichord to be played, but a gentleman there who recited Moliere and Le Cid and Shakespeare in French translations. I assure you those Belgian translations were something to remember. I think I have a record of them: I had them before.

But there was a blond girl nearby. The manager, the owner of the circus, had this gorgeous daughter, blond, blue-eyed, straight as a sword blade. Magnificent person, she was.

Well she came to me one day with a piece of music, published music about that big— a square— a two and a half or three inch square. At the bottom of it I saw "Copyright G. Schirmer, New York City." That was my publisher! I said, "Where did you get it?" She said, "I detached it from something."

On the basis of this tiny scrap of music— I don't know who wrote the original music, the composer's name, the poet's name, none of it was there. We went to work, she and I together. And we dug it out and in French we wrote a poem, and finally it was translated into Walloonese and then back into English. And after the girl sang the song it was never heard of again. It gathered dust until Jackie discovered it in my files.

The English translation is "Unused I am to lovers, I am very young. Though my heart is not unmoved, my song of love's unsung." In French it makes a wonderful collection of lines. I was wondering if it would get beyond the top of the harpsi- chord that night. She was well known for— well, the boys were all given to her enormously. When the girl came out and sang these lines the first time, the young men in the audience threw their hats in the air. The ceiling practically came down.

In one of our earliest rehearsals, Johnnie showed us this wonderful song. I immediately fell in love with it. Johnnie showed me how to sing all the embellishments and trills which are not in the original manuscript. The song is pure and sweet in its melodic line, which suits the girl's singing about her innocence. When I assisted with the editing for the Schirmer publication of this song, I recorded the embellishments as Johnnie had taught them to me. I believe I sang "Unused I Am To Lovers" at every one of my Niles concerts.

Johnnie told another wonderful World War I story about "Written in the Stars," a very romantic love song.

JJN: I wrote "Written in the Stars"— at least I did the

lyrics then— in collaboration with a young Italian. We were in a little old foxhole on Marne, on that bend in the Marne. The Germans were over our head that morning and they went back the next morning.

It was a magnificent night out there— stars, stars, stars. And this young man said to me, "I'd like to write my girl's name in the stars." All of a sudden a poem appeared to me and the two of us put it together. After that morning I never saw him again. "If I had kissed you lightly, with caution ever near... then I would have no memories, my heart would have no scars, and I would never, ever have written your name in the stars."

It is important to perform these love songs from the perspective of the character who is singing, for Johnnie habitually conceived of the dramatic elements of a song. I play a different role with each song, so that I can "sing it from the heart."

JJN: There is no doubt about a love song that has to do with a girl waking in the morning and finding her lover still there. He didn't escape during the night to parts unknown. I have discovered by looking at the audiences where this song was sung, that the so-called "bald-headed row" loves it and loves it and loves it— the idea of the girl being so fortunate that the man did not escape!

The composed love songs were always popular with audiences, and some of them I sang at almost every concert: "Unused I Am to Lovers," "Go Way From My Window," "My Lover Is a Farmer Lad," "The Wild Rider," and "Black Is the Color."

JJN: "My Lover Is a Farmer Lad." One night I called on long-distance telephone to Schirmer's in New York City. Gladys Swarthout wanted very much to have a song with a Spanish quality to it if possible— something South American. They didn't have a single suggestion for text, they didn't have a suggestion for melodic material— they just wanted a song. Well.

Of recent date I had been involved in the Grant Street Follies and there we had a burlesque Spanish dancer. Imagine! The tune went Ta Tum Tata Tum. And the next morning I went over and over it in my mind and here it was. The song was there! And Gladys sang the song.

Then Gladys went out of her apartment house, stepped on an icy place on the street, fell and broke her kneecap, and never again did she go on the concert stage. I had hoped that she would. Perhaps when she went to Spain that she would recover enough to do performances of it in France and England at least. But she died, God rest her, and the song gathered dust.

My song slept alone until Jackie came along.

As you may imagine, I have always felt privileged to be in the line of succession to "the great and glamorous Gladys Swarthout," as Johnnie called her. The character in the song is being wooed by many suitors, including "the keeper of the public house" and "one of His Majesty's most magnificent dragoons." But she loves her farmer lad because his hands are strong, his hair is tousled, and his manner is "debonair." The refrain is a kind of a tango, and it is great fun to sing.

Another great favorite is "The Wild Rider." It is one of the few up-tempo songs that Johnnie composed, so I like to interpose it between some of the slower and gentler pieces, just for variety. The woman in this song is in love with a cowboy who rides wild horses, but he'll "give it all up for his love of me." For years he promises to give up his "buckin' bronco," but he never does. She grows angrier and angrier through the song, and finally advises women to stay away from "the cowmen who swing the rawhide:" they'll leave you in the spring to ride "the buckin' bronco." It's an American cowboy art song, a waltz that gets more and more frenzied. Johnnie told a wonderful wild story about the inspiration for "The Wild Rider" at a concert in 1968, so I will share it here.

JJN: In Carpenteria, California one night I had done a performance up the road some seventy or eighty miles, and I ran away from the people who had produced the performance because they bored me. And here I was in my tailcoat and white tie with a top hat and a selection of music. A truck driver came by and I waved him down, and he of course told me later that he thought it was a Hollywood trick.

I rode and rode and rode for miles, and we stopped at places and ate and drank and had a wonderful time all the way down. We came to Carpenteria and I said, "I want to get off here." He said, "They'll kill you here— they'll just eat you up. Those women in there, they'll just pull your clothes off." I said, "That's not a bad idea, I guess."

So I went in this place. It was a place where lettuce cutters danced the night away drinking tequila which was undoubtedly dilute gasoline. I went in there and I sang and they sang and they thought it was pretty swell. Among them was a bearded, sad, heaven-bereft fellow from Boston who had rushed out there because he thought a girl was in a delicate condition— to get away from it all. And he found out that he had deserted Harvard and a career in the State Department for nothing.

He had a guitar and he sang the saddest things you ever heard. And among them was this thing, "My Lover is a Rider." "Wild horses rides he, but he's going to quit because of his love of me." Of course I had to pull it together a little bit before we could go around singing it in my programs.

When he told the story again to the girls at Agnes Scott, it was a little different: there was no truck driver, no Harvard guitar player, just the dancing lettuce cutters.

JJN: I did a little slumming in a cafe where the lettuce cutters sang and danced. It was a fabulous thing. I thought I heard something about "My lover is a rider, wild horses rides he." I doubt if there was a word of it sung there, or if a note of it was ever conceived in that place, but that's the way the imagination is. I went on to Los Angeles that night and wrote down much of it before morning.

127

One of the most controversial, and certainly the most famous, of Johnnie's songs was "Black Is the Color Of My True Love's Hair." It was controversial because Johnnie insisted that he had written the music, though not the words, while some critics insisted that he had not. He told the story over and over, with small variations that changed the emphasis slightly, but he always stoutly claimed the tune. I had no reason to disbelieve him. I had watched Johnnie compose for a long time: I knew exactly how he worked. In any case, he told the story at a recital in 1968, again at his birthday concert in Cincinnati in 1969, and once again in 1970.

> *JJN: I went with my father, now dead, God rest him, to the mountains to the city of Airy in Knott County, to a political jamboree. And there we were entertained mostly because Papa had been somewhat in a small way instrumental in getting one of the local boys out of the Atlantic. That is the Atlantic jail. They made alcoholic beverages without the benefit of the federal tax. They did all kinds of things opposed to the law. They were not law abiding. They did not think the laws existed for them. They felt that the laws were for somebody else. I feel very much the same way.*

> *While there, I heard "Black Is the Color Of My True Love's Hair." And I wrote it down and sang it for my father. My father, who had excellent judgment, said, "Never sing that song for me again. Go home, you're a smart boy, and write me a tune that's worthy of the text."*

> *I wrote it all down here, I took it to France, I sang it to the people during the war, and I sang it at the Conservatory of Music. And NOBODY paid any attention to me— because it did not end on "Do."*

> *That was a long while ago and we have learned a lot since then. I'm so stubborn, I wouldn't give up. I wouldn't give up my song for anybody or anybody's Conservatory. Nowadays "Black Is the Color of My True Love's Hair" is public property to the world and all these little girls with the*

*straggling hair and the unwashed faces try to sing my song
and tell me how it ought to be done. And I am amused
because I've got to the point in my life where I do not hate
anything or anybody, and I can't hate them. So let them
sing it in their own cockeyed way. Here is a girl who sings it
like a classic. Okay, let's have it.*

At his birthday concert the next year the story was a little
different.

*JJN: In 1916 I went with my father on a political junket to
Perry County in Kentucky, where he was going to make a
series of speeches to encourage the people to vote the way he
wanted them to vote. Well, we sang and danced: they sang,
they danced. I just listened and ate food and got sick at my
stomach. I never saw so much food and so much drink in
one group of people in all my life.*

*Among them was a little wispy fellow who sang "Black Is
the Color of My True Love's Hair." I wrote it down and
sang it to my father later. My father who came to his
conclusions like that!* [with a snap of the fingers] *said,
"Don't sing that song to me again. Take it away and write a
tune that is worthy of that wonderful text." So all of 1916,
17 (United States Army), and 18 and 19 I wrote on it. And,
as I say, I brought it back here in 1919 and they laughed as I
sat down to the piano! The laugh is on the other side of the
face now!*

*I know that many of you people have sung this song now,
and you know it. So don't be embarrassed to sing right
along with me if you like.*

He was a little sharper when he told the story again the
next year.

*JJN: "Black Is the Color of My True Love's Hair." I wrote
the tune in 1916 to please my father. It has been pushed
around quite a lot since then. It has been discovered in odd
places. Folklore collectors in the east have found it under the
arches of the bridges in Central Park. In that waste place,*

out beyond the tunnels going into Newark, into those places
where they eat hogs, I'm told that there is a man out there
with a guitar singing "Black Is the Color of My True Love's
Hair." And the young people go out and write it down, and
then they have made a folklore discovery. It was not popular
for a long while because it did not end on "do," but times
have changed.

In March of 1978, we were scheduled for a concert, but at
the last minute Johnnie lost his voice. I filled in for the
whole thing: it was the first time I had ever done that.

Johnnie was completely recovered by May of 1978 for a
concert at North Central Technical College in Mansfield,
Ohio. He was in fine fettle. I remember that we all went to
McDonald's for a meal. Johnnie was wearing his cape
with the red lining— this black wool cape had once be-
longed to Rena's father, who had been head of the rail-
roads in Russia. Whenever Johnnie appeared in this cape,
everyone stared at us: he loved that part! Rena and
Nancie and I were very hungry and we tucked into our
food. But Johnnie was in a mood to be critical and complained loudly about the food. "I would not feed this to
my dog Rosie!"

There was a Greek wedding going on at the hotel where
we stayed. It was an all-night party, and none of us could
sleep. It was on this trip, which was so much like our
other tours, that Johnnie told me flat out that I must learn
to play the dulcimer— and, as I mentioned before, I refused. Johnnie was now eighty six years old and still
going strong. I never dreamed that this would be my last
public performance with Johnnie.

Rena wrote of Johnnie's last concert in the fall of 1978, at a
performance at Warren Wilson College in Swannanoa,
North Carolina. She told, in an article for *High Roads Folio*,
a Kentucky magazine, how Johnnie stepped forward at the
end of the concert and suddenly said, "Ladies and gentlemen, in years to come you will be able to tell your children
and grandchildren that you attended John Jacob Niles' last

concert, because, my friends, this is it. So goodnight and God bless you." (HRF 1968 38). He then sang his encore, "Amazing Grace".

I began teaching at Eastern Kentucky University in the fall of 1979, an affiliation that was to last for the next thirteen years. The next year, in 1980, Johnnie's health began to decline. For a while he used a walker, and then he required a wheelchair. There were many times that he seemed to be in so much pain that at times I felt that he wasn't with us.

We made two recordings during that period, one of Niles songs and the other of Niles-Merton songs. Rena brought Johnnie in his wheelchair wherever she went, and I had a powerful sense, as we were recording the Niles-Merton songs, that Johnnie was following every note and every syllable. There was something in his eyes that told me he was attentive and concentrating, even though he was not able to communicate in the usual way.

On the first of March, 1980, I received a phone call from Rena telling me that Johnnie had passed away. Tom and John Ed were flying in from Washington, D.C., and I went to meet their plane. There was a funeral service at St. Hubert's Episcopal Church in Athens, where Johnnie had carved the church doors. Everyone met outside the church in tears. The only music was provided by the organ—there was no singing at the service. "I Wonder as I Wander" was the recessional.

My own memorial to Johnnie was the concert I gave at Eastern Kentucky University a year later, in April of 1981. Gifford Theater was full that night. I remember that after the concert, there was a long line of people from the Green Room all the way to the back of the lobby waiting to congratulate us. At my suggestion, a very special arrangement of "Amazing Grace" which Johnnie gave me before his death was performed by the University Singers. I sang the solo line. Johnnie, Nancie and I always ended our concerts with "Amazing Grace," and when Janelle was accompanying me, we used a different tune to "Amazing Grace." This choral version was, I thought, an appropriate conclusion to the memorial concert. Johnnie would have approved.

John Jacob Niles
outdoors at Boot Hill Farm with dulcimer
Photographer: Jack Cobb
Photo taken: 1960 ©

IX

Johnnie's Legacy

I had no plans to continue giving Niles concerts after Johnnie died. Nancie Field and I did editorial work preparing the manuscripts of the Niles Merton songs over 1980-1981: the Niles-Merton Songs was published in 1982 by the Mark Foster Music Company, with a beautiful preface entitled "As I Remember" by Rena.

It was a nice surprise when in January of 1982 we were invited by Eugenia Glover, the festival director of the St. Stephens Episcopal Church Festival of Music, to perform a concert of Niles songs in New Harmony, Indiana. I had met her at the time of our first concert with Johnnie in this historic place. I remembered her as a delightful person and a fine organist. At that time, Johnnie had gotten carried away and forgotten where he was supposed to be in the program, so he just kept going. He had done that before. Sometimes he just had an urge to add something to the program, so he did. But this time, I almost suspected him of forgetting that he had brought me along! Nancie and I were waiting our turn in a room where people could retreat to pray: there were candles and a statue of the Virgin Mary, and it was chilly. Johnnie must have been an hour behind in the program, so I was frantically trying to calculate what I would cut from my part. I told friends later that I thought I was going to lose my faith sitting back there, increasingly certain that he'd forgotten about me. Then finally Johnnie brought me out: the place was packed, and people were even sitting on the floor. I proposed making cuts in my part of the program but the audience wouldn't hear of it. They were totally caught up in the program, and didn't want to miss a bit of it.

New Harmony, Indiana is an historic place. Its association with music festivals for so many years only adds to its special attractions. Originally settled by Harmonists, a utopian group, in 1814, the town was sold to another social philosopher, Robert Owen, and a philanthropist named William Maclure. They invited scientists and teachers to be a part of their idealistic community.

It was on this first visit, when we performed with Johnnie, that we met Jane Owen. Her husband is a direct descendent of Robert Owen. She was very friendly and gregarious, and soon invited us to a party at her home. I believe that Jane Owen keeps a lively interest in maintaining the community's interest in educational and cultural activities. Great American architects have been invited to design futuristic buildings for New Harmony. One of my favorites is the splendid "Roofless Church" by Philip Johnson, and another is the stunning building designed by Richard Myer. Helm and I visited New Harmony not too long ago, and we were just checking into one of the elegant Shaker style guest houses at the hotel there, when we saw Jane Owen driving down the road toward us in an unusual electric car-- a little like a golf cart. She welcomed us warmly, and once again invited us to a gathering at her home.

But one of our first performances without Johnnie, as I said, was in 1982 when Rena, Nancie and I were invited to give a performance of Niles songs. Johnnie's music seems so appropriate in New Harmony, in this historical setting.

We were as cordially received as when Johnnie was with us. In fact, it seemed as though Johnnie was with us, if only in spirit.

It continued to be a busy year. I offered two workshops on Johnnie's music, one at Northern Kentucky University and another at Eastern Kentucky University. As a kind of special honor for the latter of the two workshops, Rena hosted a recital and reception at Boot Hill featuring the students who had been involved. I gave a concert at Midway College where one of my students, Wayne Gebb, had joined the faculty. As I explained in an earlier chapter, I was giving countless dulcimer performances.

In 1983 Rena gave the Niles collection to the University of Kentucky. This included not only the dulcimers but also a hundred and thirty boxes of manuscripts of correspondence and notebooks and eighty-eight boxes of manuscripts of music and plays. I sang in the program given to honor the occasion, at the Concert Hall at the University of Kentucky, on the twentieth of April.

I was invited to perform some of the Niles Merton songs at Bellarmine College that summer, as part of an Elderhostel being offered by the Thomas Merton Studies Center. A colleague and friend of mine from Eastern Kentucky University, Roe Van Boskirk, accompanied me in this performance. I particularly remember how interested he was in the Merton poems: he studied them carefully before the performance, and it seemed to me at the time that his interpretation somehow made the songs seem entirely fresh and new to me. Roe accompanied me again in a performance of a song composed by another good friend and colleague from Eastern Kentucky University, Richard Bromley. Richard's music is written in a twelve-tone scale and can be exceedingly difficult to sight-read, but Roe's expertise and bravado carried the day. It was such a pleasure to work with Roe: I believe he was one of the most talented pianists ever to come to this area. When he died of AIDS several years later, it was a great loss.

COMMUNITY PERFORMANCES

By 1983 my performances of Niles material had branched off into three categories. First were the "community" concerts, which I thought of as the bread-and-butter of Johnnie's appeal. He was never happier or more at home than when he was singing to a crowd of people in a school gymnasium or a park or a church basement or a club hall. As he often said, his music came from the people and his father had taught him that it must be returned to the people. So I sang in nursing homes and hospitals, and we performed at church banquets of all kinds, meetings of the Kiwanis and Rotary Clubs, any number of women's clubs from the Lexington Philharmonic Ladies' Guild to the DAR to the University of Kentucky Women's Club. Rena was always there, often speaking briefly of Johnnie, introducing the songs with some of his anecdotes, or reading the poetry-- always right there, beaming at me, from her seat in the front row.

We sang for the Dearborn Highland Arts Council of Lawrenceberg, Indiana. This concert had been arranged by Mary Joe Leeds, a close friend of Johnnie's and Rena's over many years. She had been a violinist with the Lexington Philharmonic Orchestra, and was a well-known performer in the area. The Arts Council had devised a pretty red program with a photo of me holding a dulcimer: we performed in the Hillforest Mansion, an elegant old home overlooking the Ohio River. Johnnie would have been happy to know about that performance, he had always been so fond of Mary Joe.

Johnnie seemed to be with us, in spirit, if you will, hovering near Nancie at the piano or sitting in the front row. I had been truly privileged over the years to have worked so closely with Johnnie-- and to have learned such a tremendous amount about the way he thought as a poet and a composer and a performer-- that it would be impossible for me to sing his material without his "presence" informing every detail of my performance. So when I sang for "the people," I remembered everything he had taught me.

Some of these concerts seemed to be commemorative in some way. For example, Rena decided to give Johnnie's piano to their musician son John Ed, and in September of 1985 she arranged one last concert of Niles songs at Boot Hill. This was an emotional occasion for me (and for many of the Niles' friends who attended), for I realized how much of a role Johnnie's beautiful piano had played in my life: it had been at the heart of so much of my education and experience.

Not long afterward, in November of 1985, we were invited to perform in one of a series of concerts dedicating the new organ at the First Presbyterian Church in Hilton Head, South Carolina. Wayne Lenke, the organist there, was responsible for arranging this series of concerts. My sister Ruth Trumbo lives in Hilton Head, and she made this a most enjoyable trip. She took us on some sightseeing tours including Savannah, Georgia, and arranged for us to appear on a local radio show to promote the concert. The audience for this concert was outstanding: they were knowledgeable and enthusiastic.

Finally in December of 1985 we were invited to my home town of Russell, Kentucky, to give a concert of Niles songs in place of a morning worship service at Mead Memorial Methodist Church. This was a wonderful experience for me personally, because my mother had been the pianist there when I was just a baby. My sister, Jeannine Stephens, invited me to sing-- Jeannine is the pianist there now. In fact, I sang my first public performance there when I was three years old-- "I Will Make You Fishers of Men." This occasion was like a reunion for me, since so many close friends from my school days came to the concert, and everyone enjoyed Johnnie's music.

Very few singers, I would imagine, have had the opportunity to work as closely with a composer as I have. I've observed the composition process of many of these works. I've "tried out" countless variations for Johnnie before he settled on a final version-- I've been told exactly how something should be sung. I've had the ambiguities of the poetry explained to me, I've been taught precisely how a word should be pronounced, and how important it is to understand all of the text and subtext involved in a piece. For me each song carries a full cargo of such information, and that information has been carefully imprinted in my consciousness by years of instruction, in rehearsals and countless performances. I cannot sing a Niles song without this memory-awareness which reaches far beyond my mind into my very nerve endings and muscles.

WORKSHOP PERFORMANCES

The second category of my Niles performances was oriented toward musicians, teachers of music and vocal students: I place the New Harmony festivals into this category, and the Kentucky Music Teachers Association conferences, as well as National Association of Teachers of Singing (NATS). These are the "conservatory audiences"-- the kind that could make Johnnie so much more nervous than when he was singing "for the people." Conservatory audiences do not bother me at all. I have always enjoyed doing workshops and vocal clinics, and I feel at home in the company of fellow teachers. More than anything, I believe, I enjoy working with the students.

In the winter of 1986, Rena, Nancie and I were invited by Kenneth Kohlenberg to Westmar College in LeMars, Iowa, where I was to give a workshop on singing Johnnie's songs. I had met Kenneth Kohlenberg at a NATS convention and given him one of my brochures, and that is how Rena and I came to find ourselves in Iowa in the midst of a snowy, snowy day. The weather made Rena nervous, and she worried whether we would have any audience at all for the performance that night. I was too busy working with the students to worry about snow.

I remember being very impressed on the one hand with how well prepared the students were, and on the other hand with how difficult it was to draw them out. Perhaps they were shy, but at first it seemed as though they were afraid to show any emotion, so I was working hard to loosen them up so that they could sing from the heart, as Johnnie always wanted. They warmed up and were truly eager for my suggestions, and it proved to be a happy experience. We all went back to the motel for a brief rest, and then we returned to campus for the concert. Despite the blizzard, there was a full house, which was truly gratifying. Westmar is a small college with a small music department, but they were ambitious and accomplished a great deal. I later heard that they had travelled to Europe.

Later that year, in October, we traveled to Georgia for two engagements. The first was a presentation at the University of Georgia, part of a musicology lecture series. Dr. Almonte Howell, a good friend of ours, was there, and I remember that he was having difficulties with cancer therapy. Dr. Howell had been the organist at the Second Presbyterian Church in Lexington when he was at the University of Kentucky. We gave our performance in a big auditorium, and I had the distinct feeling that the students had never heard of John Jacob Niles. Johnnie could always handle that sort of thing by saying, "Now, children" and telling a story about the past, but I was a little unnerved. For some reason, I was reminded of my days in school, sitting in a big auditorium and being polite while some elderly person talked to us about things from ancient history. This time I was the elderly person. It was unsettling.

Nancie and I packed up after the University of Georgia performance and drove right up into the mountains to a school in Young Harris, Georgia. As night fell we encountered some very thick fog that made driving downright scary, but we arrived safely at our destination. The fog did not break until midmorning the next day, and when it did we were awestruck by the beauty of this place.

After a day of rest we joined the faculty and students at supper, which was great fun because they were having a contest to see who could decorate the best pumpkin (it was the day before Halloween). Our Young Harris evening was quite the opposite of the University of Georgia experience. When the students came to the dining hall, they left all their belongings-- books, jackets, sweaters-- on the porch outside, almost as if this were a summer camp. I had a wonderful conversation with a teacher and writer whose name was Betty: I am ashamed that I didn't record her full name at the time. We read Thomas Merton's poetry together and had a marvelous evening. Being a performer is like being an adventurer: there are so many surprises along the way that one eventually learns to "expect the unexpected."

I was working in 1987 on the new G. Schirmer edition of *The Songs of John Jacob Niles*, which included eight songs that had never been published before. I had the manuscript copies of the songs, and Johnnie's invaluable instruction on how they should be performed. It was interesting work, editing this music for publication, attending to all the details.

It was an honor to be invited by the Smithsonian Institution to give a Niles concert during the American Music Week celebration of the Smithsonian Resident Associates' Program. This concert was held in the National Museum of Natural History's Baird Auditorium. Ralph Rinzler, the musicologist, introduced us. John Ed Niles lives in the Washington area-- he is the conductor of the Opera Theater of Northern Virginia-- and he joined with Rena in providing the narratives and anecdotes introducing the individual songs. Then Nancie Fields' daughter, Gwen Sither, gave a delightful reception at her home after the concert.

I have saved and treasured a very kind thank-you note I received from Marc Overton following the Smithsonian concert. "Once again," he wrote, "I repeat my gratitude to you for your work in assembling the program. . . for your superb artistry and deep humanity in communicating this great music to our audience."

Three years later, when *The Songs of John Jacob Niles* was published, G. Schirmer sponsored another Washington concert to dedicate the new book. Peter Herb, the director of special projects at G. Schirmer, made the arrangements. Henry Burroughs, a baritone who performs a great deal in the Washington area, joined Nancie and me to sing several of Johnnie's gambling songs. The eight "new" songs-- I'd been singing them for a long time by now-- were "My Lover is a Farmer Lad," "Wild Rider," "Ribbon Bow," "Little Black Star," "The Robin and the Thorn," "Unused I am to Lovers," "When I Get Up Into Heaven," and "The Flower of Jesse." This concert was held in the Arts Club of Washington, which had once been the private home of President Monroe. It was a charming setting. I enjoyed meeting Andy Kaplan Herb, Peter Herb's wife, and the audience was welcoming and enthusiastic.

NILES-MERTON PERFORMANCES

The third category of performances involves the Niles-Merton songs in particular. In 1984 I was invited to perform at Holy Cross Monastery in Westpark, New York. My accompanist was to be Nancy Roth, whom I had never met: Nancy was an Episcopal minister and a graduate of my alma mater, Oberlin College. She worked at Trinity Episcopal Church in New York City. I was taken to Nancy's home first-- it was a lovely artistic house-- before she took me on a tour of Scarsdale. We hit it off immediately.

I was totally intrigued by the monastery and by monastery life. I made some notes in a little notebook so I would remember this experience. The monks only "owned the cross around their necks," I wrote. "Each one had his own task, like cooking or making miniature furniture." I also made a point of going to all the services during my visit there.

After the recital, the monks gave a wine and cheese party for us, and I was truly honored that they enjoyed the music as much as they did. They were genuinely affectionate in their reception. Their response reminded me of Thomas Merton's frankly emotional reaction upon hearing this music.

So you can understand that I was thrilled to be invited to sing at Holy Cross once again in June of 1985. This time Nancy Roth and I practiced at St. James Church. We were met at New Paltz by a Canadian monk, who brought us to lunch at the monastery. The food was outstanding: I remember that we had manicotti. I also remember copying down into my little notebook the words of the blessing given before the meal. (It occurred to me later that, had he been there, Johnnie would have been intrigued by this blessing too, and would have done exactly the same thing I did). Next, Father Brown gave us a tour of Holy Cross, and then we went to Vespers and listened to the Gregorian chant. I remember that when I took the sacrament the monks kissed me: it was very moving. I could hear Johnnie saying, *"I am not a Catholic. If anything, I am a Zen Buddhist."* Johnnie would have loved to have come to Holy Cross and said that.

My room had a lovely single bed in it. From the window I could see a view of the summer mists of the beautiful Hudson River valley. In the morning we were awakened very early: Matins was held at 6:30 A.M. There was a quiet knock on my door, then the greeting, "Thanks be to God." It was a rainy morning and the monks served us a great breakfast. Nancy Roth and I had a little time to rehearse before the Merton program began.

"I enjoy the pace, a dance," I wrote in my journal. The monks had a large black dog named Sophie. She looked like a Labrador, I thought. Sophie was everywhere. She

was the kind of the dog that liked to lie down in the door-
way or on the landing of the stairs, just to be in the middle
of things. I took a four or five mile hike with Margaret
Betts. "Wonderful slow dropping rain." "Complete silence
will begin with new people coming in. Singing for the
silent ones."

Father Bernard Van Ways talked to us about Thomas
Merton. This was followed by a question and answer
period. My notes continue, "Sister St. John lives as a
solitary. Two woodcarvings." I remember Father Bernard
reading the poetry before the songs. When we finished the
performance, there was a moment of silence that seemed
forever. Then applause. I wrote, "Final performance the
best. Dear people ask for autographs." "John DAIDO," I
wrote, "a Zen Buddhist, was a real trip."

In 1986 my friend Kerstin Warner invited me to perform
Niles-Merton songs for a special group-- a Kentucky
Endowment for the Humanities seminar for teachers at
Eastern Kentucky University that was studying American
autobiography: they had read *Seven Storey Mountain* as an
example of spiritual autobiography, and they were eager to
learn more about Merton. The teachers' seminar joined
forces with EKU's Creative Writing seminar, led at the time
by Bill and Dorothy Sutton, and so there was a poetry
reading by Robert Hedin, a North Carolina poet, as half of
the program. There were half a dozen nuns in the audience from Saint Mark's School, who had been invited by
one of the teachers in the seminar, Sister Maria Francine
Stacy. Rena was there to read the poetry, and Nancie
demonstrated the block of wood Johnnie had made for the
accompaniment of "Ohio River." There was a reception at
which I had a chance to talk to Robert Hedin about his
poetry as well as Thomas Merton's.

I was very pleasantly surprised a few months later when
Robert Hedin telephoned me from North Carolina to
propose a "Merton day" at the Reynolda House Museum
of American Art in Winston-Salem, and to invite us to

perform the Niles-Merton songs. I recommended that Michael Mott, Merton's biographer, be invited as well, and on March 28, 1987 the event took place. Rena and Nancie and I were housed right in the historic museum, our rooms surrounded by a magnificent collection of paintings. My uncle William Morrow took us out to dinner at the Forsythe Country Club the day before the concert. Our performance was very well received. (In fact, Marjorie Northup, the curator of Reynolda House invited us back to perform in November 1989. My accompanist at that time, Claire Vance, and I had prepared a program of Gershwin and Porter songs. This was a late-evening performance-- eleven P.M.-- and Claire played solo Scott Joplin. It was quite a change of pace from my Niles concerts, and we had great fun).

As soon as we came back to Kentucky from the Merton day, within just a matter of days, I gave a solo recital at Asbury College in Wilmore, Kentucky. I had taught for a year, part-time, at Asbury, and it was marvelous to see the faculty and friends there again. I remember my students there with great affection because they were very serious about their education. They truly seemed to have come to college to learn.

Shortly after that I performed Niles music again in the Special Collections and Archives section of the University of Kentucky Library. Jim Birchfield, the Editor of the Kentucky *Review,* and also the Assistant Director for Collection Development, was instrumental in arranging this recital. A special edition of the *Kentucky Review* that year was dedicated to Thomas Merton, "A Thomas Merton Symposium." My friend Kerstin had written one of the articles in this issue, "'For Me Nothing Has Ever Been the Same:' Composing the Niles-Merton Songs, 1967-1970," based on my experiences working with Johnnie. As usual, I had a very responsive and enthusiastic audience. Rena provided the narrative material: I remember noticing that the place where I sat waiting "in the wings" was an area dedicated to housing the archives of the retiring President of the University of Kentucky, Otis Singletary. It's odd how vividly I remember details about the place where I wait to perform: my adrenalin must be high.

Audiences who are familiar with the works of Thomas Merton are always very special-- they seem to be open to both the contemporary sound of the Niles art songs and to the spiritual quotient of the poetry. Dr. Anne Page Brooks of the Humanities Department at Eastern Kentucky University had invited us to perform Niles songs for a conference of the Integrative Studies Association, and she was particularly fascinated by the Niles-Merton songs. A casual conversation led to her setting up a "Merton day" at the Boone Tavern Hotel in nearby Berea, Kentucky.

There was quite a special crowd at this gathering, including a number of the monks from Gethsemani. Brother Patrick Hart spoke, as did Michael Mott and others, and then Nancie, Rena and I presented a number of the Niles-Merton songs. So many people were there who keep the memory of Thomas Merton alive through their continuing study. Dear old friends of Johnnie and Rena's (and ours) were there, including Hanna Shepherd and her husband Bob. It was one of those audiences that seems to be holding its breath, it is so intent on the music. Someone from Berea had made a large fabric applique wall hanging-- a portrait of Thomas Merton-- which seemed to preside over the whole event.

The monks and the musicians were invited to Hanna and Bob Shepherd's home after the formalities of the day, and we had a fine party that involved good food and drink and plenty of hilarity and song. I suppose we were a pretty colorful group, the tonsured monks in their long robes and sandals, unbound by silence for the time being, belting out show tunes and whatever else anyone felt like singing. Brother Patrick Hart, Paul Quenon, and Bob Daggy, the head of Merton studies at Bellarmine College, were there, as were Tom and Nancie Field. Jim and Jeannette Cantrell, who own the Merton shop in Bardstown, were there as well.

In May of 1991, Rena, Claire Vance and I were asked to perform at a Benedictine Spirituality Conference at New Harmony, Indiana. A note from Elizabeth Swensen welcomed us and provided us with a schedule from the entire three day conference. We were to perform Johnnie's songs-- not just the Niles-Merton songs-- at eight in the evening on Wednesday the eighth.

The schedule listed "Morning Prayer" at 7:30 A.M. in the Roofless Church, followed by a Meditation led by Father Laurence. Breakfast was at 8:15, and a note said, "Begin Greater Silence through breakfast." As always, I was fascinated by the monastic discipline, so I went to the morning lecture in the Barn Abbey on the subject of "The Religious Nature of the Ego and the Soul," by Dean Pittman McGehee, and stayed for the discussion, took the Eucharist at the Roofless Church, and then had lunch at the Benedictine Conference Center. That afternoon, the schedule read "NOTHING SCHEDULED AND NOTHING EXPECTED."

After Evensong at St. Stephen's Church and dinner at the Benedictine Conference Center, we gave our concert. I sang a few songs from the new edition of the Niles songbook-- "When I Get Up Into Heaven" and "The Flower of Jesse." Then we did five Niles-Merton songs ending with the elegy "For My Brother," and concluded our program with five songs from the courtship cycle, including "Black is the Color" and "The Wild Rider."

I recently went to Gethsemani one Sunday in 1994 with my friend Evelyn Niedenzu, to go to church and visit Thomas Merton's grave. There was such a feeling of being at peace in that church. I remembered that another friend had told me that Brother Patrick Hart had told her there was more about the Niles-Merton collaboration in the "restricted jourals" of Thomas Merton— this will be published later. I wandered into the Merton shop there, saw Jim and Jeannette Cantrell, and was pleased to see the book by John Howard Griffin displayed there. I am curious to know what the restricted journals say about the music and the rehearsals, but we will have to wait.

Evelyn and I visited the grave of Thomas Merton. "FATHER LOUIS" reads the headstone of the simplest, most unassuming, quiet gravesite imaginable. I thought of "Mosaic: St. Praxed's" at the Newman Center concert that Thomas Merton never lived to hear.

So like a quiet pigeon in a hollowed rock
You stand there in the wall's curve
Made of stone needled tapestry
In this dim sheltered paradise
Mary made of love art and poetry.

Postscript

I decided in 1996 to retire from vocal performance. This was an informal decision, and thank goodness I didn't announce it to "the great world," as Johnnie might say, or arrange any grand farewell concerts, for not long after this, I received an interesting phone call with an irresistible challenge. Michael Fitzpatrick, an outstanding young cellist in this area, and pianist Loren Tice picked up on the suggestion that they get in touch with me concerning the Niles-Merton songs.

The Dalai Lama was coming to Gethsemani in July to be part of something called an "East-West Dialogue," a five day conference on the religious life. Thomas Merton had been studying Eastern monastic discipline and meditation when he left for Bangkok, and so someone suggested that the Niles-Merton songs be a part of the occasion. We previewed the songs in March before an audience of nuns and priests who were gathered at Our Lady of Grace monastery in Beech Grove, Indiana, to plan and organize details for the "East West Dialogue." We sang thirty minutes before the morning Mass in a beautiful little chapel. I was thrilled to be performing in a holy place, and the addition of the cello enhanced the depth of the songs we presented. As things transpired, this concert before the Dalai Lama never came to pass, but I can count on these little surprises coming my way.

Not too long ago, I was chatting with my friend Gay Reading about a birthday tape that Johnnie had sent to him in Viet Nam. Gay is the nephew of Caroline and Victor Hammer: he had met Thomas Merton quite a few more times than I had. I remembered making the tape at Boot Hill on Gay's birthday, August first, 1969.

> JJN: Dear Gay, You recognize my voice, I'm sure-- this is John Jacob Niles. And we're broadcasting, or rather recording, in the big music room at Boot Hill Farm. We are going to send you this tape and we hope you'll be able to play it on your little machine out there. Principally we're making a tremendous effort to get a copy of 'The Greek Women' to you, because we understand that you thought a great deal of it.

> You don't need any explanation about Merton-- or John Jacob Niles-- you know Janelle Pope and Jackie Roberts. You've heard them before right here in this room. We have in the room with us tonight Caroline [Hammer] and Mr. Agee and Mr. and Mrs. Middleton and Poot our Siamese who is great with cats. You should see her, her belly is bending down to the ground and I'm about to get her rollerskating: I'll put it under her so she can move around more easily.

> Janelle looks very lovely and so does Jackie, they're both in miniskirts. As the photographer said-- when he photographed them in this room-- the girls don't have to sing at all!

> All right, let's have it. Now the first thing we're going to do is a thing called 'Mirror's Mission.'

Gay told me that he often communicated with family and friends on small reel-to-reel tapes. He said he had received Johnnie's tape not long after his birthday. He was a Riverine in the Infantry, on a big ship, an LST, on the Mekong River. It was a base day, he said, a rare day on the ship when all the men were on board and there was a feeling of security and safety from the rockets. It was a beautiful evening after a long hot day. Gay took his tape player to the deck where he could be alone to listen to the tape.

JJN: All of the party didn't get here at once. I saw a car flying around just now containing your father and Hanna and Bob and Hanna's mother. I think the reason Hanna's late-- she has this unfortunate Continental point of view about practically everything, you know, and everything on the Continent is late, if you know what I mean.

The next item we're playing is called 'Autumn.' "Bird on branch, singing and losing leaves/ Autumn held the bow of the whimpering violin." You know, Tom Merton was given to the word 'violin.' He introduced it time after time, and I often said to him, "Tom, there were no violins in that period." He said, "Don't be such a stickler for facts."

Gay said that often as a child he had been brought to Boot Hill because he was about John Ed Niles' age, and he had always loved hearing Johnnie's music. There was nothing more wonderful than sitting on the floor with the other children, enjoying the music. Now on the Mekong River, sitting on the deck of the LST, listening to the music played for him at his birthday party on the other side of the world, he was profoundly moved. He'd told Johnnie how much he admired "The Greek Women", and so that song was featured.

JJN: In all my days and time I may never get a clearer picture than I had of the situation in "The Greek Women." I believe I like it almost as much as you do.

At this song, Gay said, he wept. "There were many of us in Viet Nam, like me, who felt strongly opposed to war, especially this war. To hear on my birthday tape these powerful peace songs was a very emotional experience. I saw Agamemnon fulfilling his karma, and Clytemnestra as an avenging angel!" "The Ohio River: Louisville," "The

Mirror's Mission," "Cana," "Wisdom," "The Lament of the Maiden," one after another, concluding with "Responsory," all of them peace songs. I rounded up some of my buddies and played the tape for them, with the same effect."

Gay said that he had known that Thomas Merton had been advised by the Vatican's Buddhist-Catholic liaison that he must pay his respects to the Dalai Lama before seeking out the elderly meditation teacher he particularly wanted to meet. So he met the Dalai Lama and was won over instantly when he said to Merton, "Oh, Rimpoche is my teacher. Perhaps before you see Rimpoche you should have a lesson." Whereupon the two men slipped to the floor to meditate together. Said Gay, "The Dalai Lama has a powerful presence, a satori."

I told Gay how we had all sat on the floor for a poetry reading on Merton's last visit, and that we had a photograph taken while Johnnie was reading his poems and Thomas Merton was happily listening. I mentioned the powerful intuition Johnnie had had the day Thomas Merton died in Bangkok: "I saw Thomas face down in water, and I knew he was dead."

Gay said he would never forget that day either. Before being sent to Viet Nam, "I'd been assigned by the army to work in the Fort Knox Library," he said, "Possibly because I had a degree-- but I will never forget the day that I heard of Thomas Merton's death on the radio. I was cleaning the floor of the library and I dropped the bucket of water I was carrying, I was so stunned by the news. I knew that I had to call home immediately." I had not heard Gay's story before, but it made me think of how so many of our lives were touched by these events, and I continue to marvel at my being a part of this history.

BIRTHDAYS WITH RENA

When my friend Rena celebrated her eightieth birthday, I was happy to be asked to sing for the celebration, just as I had sung for Johnnie's eightieth. The concert at the home of Al and Billie Winer was to be a surprise, so chairs had been set up in their recreation room on the lower level. I thought of all the concerts-- literally hundreds of them-- that Rena had set up for us, getting the programs ready, preparing the room, being responsible for the instruments and the music and all the other important details of preparation.

Tedrin Blair Lindsay was my pianist, a very talented young man whom I've enjoyed working with recently. Rena was completely surprised to be escorted downstairs, to be given a program, and to be regaled with a performance in her honor. Hanna and Bob Shepherd, Carolyn Hammer and her nephew Gay were there, as well as many other dear friends. It was a very happy occasion: I had the feeling that this was something momentous and appropriate, as though one chapter was ending and at the same time another one would be beginning. Just as at Johnnie's birthday concerts (when this year's songs were presented and yet next year's songs were always on his mind), something wonderful was completed, something had come full circle, and at the same time I was looking forward to whatever the next year would bring.

So when Rena and I were on a plane a couple of years ago, going to John Ed Niles' latest opera production at his Northern Virginia Opera Company in Washington, D.C., out of the blue she announced that she wanted to throw me a big birthday party. Rena had had birthday dinners for me before: I have one wonderful photo of Rena and me taken by our friend Billie Winer at a party she gave for me and Bob Shepherd.

This would be a big party, because she said she wanted to invite at least fifty people-- and she wanted me to perform. She made the necessary reservations at the University of Kentucky Faculty Club, and Claire Vance and I got to work on the entertainment for the program. The program was partly inspired by a pair of dresses I'd received from some good friends in Hollywood, Henry Prichard and Andy Beck. Conrad Hilton's social secretary, Olive Wakeman, had been a friend of theirs: every time a new Hilton Hotel was opened somewhere in the world, she wore a fabulous new gown. I reminded Henry and Andy of her, so they sent the dresses on to me because they thought I would have fun with them. They were right. These were magnificent dresses by famous Hollywood designers.

One gown was a multicolored fantasia of embroidered pink peonies and yellow double tulips, all hand embroidered and bejeweled with pearls and pink stones, the sort of beautiful gown that Grace Kelly might wear. We called the performance "The 'Dress' Rehearsal." I wore this pastel dress for the first part of the program, when I sang some of the folk songs with a harp accompaniment by Sally Kelton, a very talented local musician. Then Claire and I did some of Johnnie's love songs, "Written in the Stars," "My Lover is a Farmer Lad," and "Black is the Color of My True Love's Hair," concluding with "The Blue Madonna." Sally played a harp piece by Lara, while I changed costume.

The little black dress was so glamorous I could never imagine wearing it myself: I had to have a "character" who would wear it in a "performance," so I could live up to that dress. This was a cocktail dress with skinny straps, all covered with black sequins. Six horizontal rows of black bead fringe made this perfect for the Sondheim and Gershwin portion of Claire's and my repertoire. The Big Finish was built around the fact that this black gown "moved" so spectacularly. We had decided to surprise Henry Prichard by performing the song he wrote, "Kentucky." And to put the final touches on this number, I secretly asked one of my friends, Billy Breed, to teach me a tap dance. I should say he taught me how to fake a little tap dance.

We had such a great time just preparing for this birthday party, that I must remember to write about the actual party, because I want to end this book by honoring Rena, recall-

153

ing the wonderful times we had. So instead of concluding with her passing, I want to raise a champagne glass to this memory. Fifty people were indeed there, our harp pieces had been properly celestial, and Claire and I were having a fine time with our "nightclub" songs. Then I surprised everyone by opening Helm's briefcase and changing into my tap shoes. (Not even Helm knew I was going to dance!) I came out tapping and singing "Soon I'll be goin' where the soft breeze is blowin' in Kentucky." Ham that I am, I wound up the song in Jolson style, on my knees, arms lifted up, looking at the sky. I have to say we brought down the house-- it was a smashing success. Rena believed that I had gone and learned tap dancing just for this occasion!

For this wonderful party, and for all of the wonderful times, I want to conclude with this tribute. To Rena Niles, the dearest and most loyal of friends through all our years together. I know you and Johnnie are always right there in the front row, in spirit, whatever I do. Therefore I offer the last word in this book as a toast-- join me-- to Rena!

☾

Left to right: Janice Pope, John Jacob Niles,
Jacqueline Roberts and Thomas Mertin
at Boot Hill Farm
Photographer: Helm Roberts
Photo taken: 1968 ©

Index

The Authors

Kerstin P. Warner is the author of Thomas Otway, a critical biography of the Restoration playwright who was considered "next to Shakespeare," and The Home, the libretto for an opera about a murderer in a nursing home, with music composed by Richard Bromley. Her article on Jacqueline Roberts and John Jacob Niles, "'For Me Nothing Has Ever Been the Same:' Composing the Niles-Merton Songs, 1967-1970" appeared in The Kentucky Review, Vol. VII, No. 2, in 1987.

A graduate of Vassar College with M.A. and Ph.D. from the University of Minnesota, she has taught at the University of Minnesota and is currently a Professor of English at Eastern Kentucky University, where she met Jackie Roberts and began work, over lunch in the cafeteria, on this book. Her interests in music, dramatic literature, and poetry— and the ways in which they converge— are reflected in much of her work, which includes The Noblest Frailty of the Mind: a Study of Dryden's Heroines and the Passions of the Soul, Thomas Otway's Strumpet Fortune, translations of Moliere, and the poetry for Five Songs by Richard Bromley.

Kerstin Warner lives with her husband John Warner, a Professor of Linguistics with special interest in computer languages, in Richmond Kentucky. Their daughter Kerstin is following the family tradition of teaching Gifted and Talented students in Westport, Connecticut, and their daughter Sarah is currently Director of Development for En-semble Theatre of Cincinnati.

Jacqueline Roberts is well-known in the Bluegrass area for her long association with John Jacob Niles and for her extensive performing and teaching career. She edited The Songs of John Jacob Niles, published by the Mark Foster Music Company in 1982, selecting and editing the last eight songs in that edition.

A graduate of Oberlin Conservatory of Music with a M.M. from Miami University of Oxford Ohio, she was adjunct professor at Asbury College, and for thirteen years adjunct professor at EKU.

She is a member of National Association of Teachers of Singing, a Charter member of Lexington Federated Music Club, and a member of the National Society of Arts and Letters, Kentucky Chapter. Professionally, she sang with the Roger Wagner Chorale in California. She has done summer theatre at Cain Park Theatre in Cleveland, Ohio. She was one of the charter members of the Lexington Musical Theatre, and also served on the Board of that organization. In her private studio, Ms. Roberts has taught many young voice students, preparing them with an "Audition for College"to go on to study at colleges and universities all over the country.

Jacqueline Roberts lives with her husband Helm Roberts, best known as an architect-planner in Lexington, Kentucky. Helm Roberts is notable as the designer of the unique Kentucky Vietnam War Memorial, a sundial with a gnomon that touches the name of the deceased on the day that they were killed. Her son Bruce is President of the Carolina Financial Group of Brevard, North Carolina, and her son John is a Veterinarian who spent two years in the Peace Corps in Nepal.

Colophon

The publishing of this book:

A Journey With

John Jacob Niles

A Memoir of My Years With Johnnie

was produced by the University of Kentucky Libraries
in March, 2001. This book was designed by
John W. Quinn and the body text was set on a Macintosh,
in Palintino type and Corrona MT for display. Text for the
Index and Authors pages are in Garamond Condensed,
while the Colophon text is in Garamond.
The John Jacob Niles title is in University Ornate-Bold.

One thousand copies have been printed.